The Other Side
of
The Wall

MARIE MICHEAUX

Anne Dubuisson Anderson- Editor
Damon Freeman- Cover Designer
Benjamin Carrancho- Interior Formatter and Designer

ISBN- 978-0-9905001-0-0

Printed in the United Estates of America and the UK
Published August 2014
Blast Publishing LLC
75 N. Woodward Ave. #10000
Tallahassee, FL 32313

For my dear friend
James. Thank you so
much for arranging
this lovely visit to Venice—
so many beautiful buildings

In Loving Memory of

Sophie Micheaux and Jacques Corpening Martin

and mysteries still to
be discoverd. I do hope
we come back again
one day.

with lots of love from

Ellene

~~×~~

Your lady in Waiting!

FOR

Mom and Dad

TABLE OF CONTENTS

ACKNOWLEDGEMENTS

I THANK THE friends and family members who were supportive and not judgmental while I struggled through the writing of this difficult story.

Starting your life over as a single woman in a foreign country while grieving great personal losses is difficult. Just dealing with the foreign agencies for opening accounts for utilities can seem overwhelming. I am not a perfect person but I have tried very hard to become part of the Italian community. The warmth of the Italian people and the education of the Italian culture have been dear to my heart for many years. As a writer I believe it is important to be out in life "seeing" and "hearing" in order to understand people, their passions, and their culture. It is also important to allow yourself to be open and vulnerable for others to trust you with their vulnerabilities. People are what is near to their heart. Developing trust is a bond that should not be broken. I thank the people of all the cultures who have helped me and been accepting of my new life in Venice and Murano. I thank the people who essentially "gave me a break" when I may have seemed too peculiar while chatting too much and taking notes on napkins. I appreciate the kindness and patience of people as I've struggled with the Italian language and not condemning me for my slow learning of languages in general. Being a liberated American woman is not always understood and accepted by every culture. I am thankful to all the people in Italy particularly Venice and Murano who have accepted me as I am. I hope to become a better writer and person from the richness of knowledge, kindness, and understanding that you have extended to me. I love my new life here and feel very privileged to be surrounded by such great people.

"Fight the darkness
And look for the light
Always reach for the shining star
Behind the clouded night
Tutto è possibile"

— *Marie Micheaux*

PREFACE

I AM AN American woman residing in Venice, Italy. Following the death of my child and losing most of my savings in the real estate collapse, I chose to start my life over in this enchanting medieval city. This is a true story about a horrifying unexplained situation I endured involving my neighbors, soon after my move into a new flat here. Although I had never met them, they terrorized me, primarily at night, and I overheard multiple tales of their plans for me, from helping me, to abduction to murder! It became a twisted game of manipulations where I didn't know the rules or how lethal their intentions could be. I tried to confront them and I tried to run from them, but all my attempts failed. Luckily, with the aid of a few loving and empathetic "angels," I was able to break free and leave the country urgently to seek help and answers. My encounters with them began from the first day I moved into the new place and continued for just under a month, until I left. Since experiences affect people based on their life history, I include other pertinent memoirs. To protect the privacy of some of the people who were a part of the experience, I have changed their names in my writings.

Immediately following the events, I documented conversations by tape recorder and logged important data to assist in my evaluations. Obviously, it has been difficult to write and relive the trauma, but I believe for myself and from the urgings of friends, family, and a well-respected intuitive, Jonna Rae Bartges, that this profound mystery should be told.

For almost 30 years I visited Venice. Originally, I arrived as a student for a semester to study architecture with the University of Virginia. I have traveled the world since, but Venice haunts me until I return. Although it is a volatile city with the aqua alta (high water), it is perfectly precariously balanced and intertwined with culture, romance, friendships, inspiration, and passion. One year while visiting the city I met a Venetian woman who had just returned after living many years in the United States with her American husband. She warned, "There is a very big problem with Venice. Once you are a part of it, you cannot leave."

The energies of Venice are a heavy mixture of all emotions. Some are also very magical. You may be walking along a fondamenta (a path beside the water) one sunny day, and suddenly be stricken by intense feelings of love emanating from the city walls, even though you are alone. Often, upon returning to Venice, I'm brought to tears for no apparent reason as soon as I set foot on the ancient stones and begin my walk around the city. This phenomenon is often spoken about between Venetians. The energy literally reaches out and takes hold of you. In more comical ways, it's not uncommon seeing someone in an unusual outfit, like a fairy costume, prancing around town just because the mood struck her. I've always been an icing person instead of a cake person. Venice is like the icing of an exquisitely decorated, excruciatingly sweet, and passionately decadent cake. This intensity is what drew me to live in the city.

It took me many years to finally make the commitment to move here. I have felt as though I have had this torrid long-distance love affair with the city itself. After arriving at a point in my life where I was forced to start over again, I reflected upon what was important to me and what I loved. I needed balance in my life and I loved Venice. I realized I had to give into my feelings about the city, move here, and continue the relationship.

I am certain that the readers will draw their own conclusions about my story. Or perhaps some will consider how the first inhabitants of the Venetian lagoon were from the 400's AD and conclude only that my story is surely just another one of the many mysteries of Venice.

1

FROM THE BEGINNING

I GREW UP IN the mountains of Western North Carolina in a traditional, high-spirited family. My father is a well-known retired North Carolina Supreme Court Justice, who was honored several times for his contributions to society. My mother is a devoted wife and mother who encouraged us to travel and to follow our own paths. I have two older brothers, Matthew and John, both of whom have been attorneys. John's biological father was killed in a plane crash when John was very young. So my father adopted him. Later, I was adopted as an infant. I have wondered if I could be part Cherokee due to my "sensitivities" and the fact that my biological mother was from an area near Cherokee. However, my desire to know the details of my past are not important. I believe that the people who raise you or "parent you" are your parents. And the hand you are dealt is the one you are supposed to play.

One of my "sensitivities" is my acute hearing. I hear more frequencies than the average person. And I can become overwhelmed by too much noise. In houses I've lived in, I can hear when the mechanical equipment of my neighbors' properties is not working properly by the change in pitch of the units. One neighbor in particular in Miami was very grateful when I called to notify her that their pool pump was breaking down, before it flooded their property. I also telephoned the police when I overheard a conversation in the middle of the night of a man threatening another man with a gun, over two acres away. They were able to apprehend him. And, of course, there are the common annoyances when I overhear private conversations from the other side of the house. So, in a way, this sensitivity is both a blessing and a nuisance.

Even from when I was very young my mother attributes my never napping as a child to being too bothered by the afternoon noises. I still never nap in the day. She has also wondered if, when I climbed out of my crib as an infant to lie on the floor in the corner, it was due to some noise in the room or some spirit coaxing me to do this.

Another example of my hearing sensitivity is my

connection to music. I will dream of a song, wake up, and write down the entire song. Sadly, I don't remember all the music but I often retain the lyrics and part of the melody. Also, when I go to sleep with a problem on my mind, I will often wake to a song playing in my head with the lyrics explaining the situation.

As far as my other "sensitivities," I have often had prophetic dreams. And, I've been labeled "clairvoyant" (clear seeing), "clairsentient" (clear sensing), an "intuitive empath" (feeling others' emotions), and somewhat "telepathic" (thought transference with another person). Personally, I think there is too much responsibility associated with these labels and I don't really know for sure if they accurately portray me or not. I don't know the parameters of the classifications. I am not one of these new-age people who desperately want and try to be "psychic" in order to make money from readings. I just acknowledge that I am a "sensitive." I cannot call upon my gifts to occur, but they occur randomly. I use them to better myself and to help someone in need if a situation arises. I do believe everyone has a level of "psychic abilities." However, I do not believe that you can learn to be a great receiver. I think what you have is what you are gifted with at birth. You can improve your abilities if you meditate and learn to move your energy, but you cannot teach yourself to be a highly operating psychic. Well-intentioned and powerful psychics are rare.

When a close friend of mine was pregnant, I had a dream about her. I was staying at my family's isolated lake house. I dreamed she was explaining to me that she was having a baby who was half human and half Labrador retriever. Evidently, she was unable to carry a human baby to term, but was capable of carrying one that was half human and half dog. She assured me that she and her husband were very happy with their decision to do this. In the dream I reassured her that I was happy as long as she was happy. Obviously, when I awoke I was mortified. How bizarre! I was seeing my friend the next week and wasn't exactly sure if I should tell her for fear it would terrify her. But in the car coming back from the airport, I couldn't hold it in and told her.

She laughed hysterically, which was not the reaction I expected. And she said, "Just wait until you see what's on our refrigerator."

When we arrived at her apartment in Miami, she showed me a magazine clipping posted on the refrigerator. There was a picture of a child that was half dog (Labrador) and half human. The title read, "Dog-child Doing Well." She informed me that there was a party at her house and her friends were joking that she was going to have that child. I obviously tuned in and dreamed it. Actually, my friend and I have often had a connection with our dreams.

I've had many other dreams that were validated. I've dreamed of strangers I would meet in the next few days. I've also dreamed of past-life places I would later see and recognize. For instance, once I was meeting a friend who lived in a part of Los Angeles I had never visited before. The area seemed spookily familiar. It reminded me of a dream I'd had years before, where there was a lavish party in this boutique hotel overlooking a lake. The people were dressed in period clothing. I asked my friend if there was a hotel around the lake. He said, "No, it's all residential." We drove around until I recognized the view from the dream more clearly. Then I followed the road to the same perspective that I remembered. Sitting on the site was an apartment building that was a converted hotel.

I've also dreamed of disasters that would occur, including 9/11 and the Kennedy plane crash. And I've dreamed of details of places and weaponry in Iraq, and assisted a friend who was called to duty. I knew nothing of Iraq or of weaponry, but my explanations helped him when he later encountered certain situations. When he returned to the US he said, "Thank you for all the things you told me. You saved my life and the lives of my men. You were in my head the whole time."

My mother kept the household very regimented. I did well in school and played sports, particularly field hockey. I played the guitar and wrote songs, though I was focused on more seemingly practical pursuits in science and mathematics. In general I was a sweet and shy girl. However, from being in a family of very strong personalities I learned to speak up for what I believed in. I was a Tomboy and a basic all-American kid. There were some difficult and isolating times when my mother's two best friends were dying of cancer. This went on for a few years. Our house would either be very emotional or lonely when my mother was taking care of her friends' families. My father traveled often with work in the early years also. But I focused on my schooling and my writing.

I excelled in academics and went off to Hollins College a year early. After a year I transferred to the Architecture School at the University of Virginia. In my junior year at UVA a life threatening event occurred, and I believe this increased my sensitivities. A maniac with a rifle and a shotgun abducted my boyfriend and me from a parking lot. He wanted to take us to his friend's house in the country to "use" the new guns he had just stolen. Eventually, after a terrifying drive around town, my boyfriend convinced our abductor to stop for a bottle of wine, knowing that this was the last spot of civilization before we entered the back roads. He ordered me to go get the bottle. But not wanting to take too long and risk his shooting my boyfriend, I timidly confessed, "I'm not 21, I can't go … maybe he should go." Dumbfounded by my response, he lost his focus and lowered the gun just below the seat height. My boyfriend grabbed the gun and pushed it down further to the floor as he climbed over into the back seat with him. We all struggled as the back door was slung open. I was handed off one of the guns, which I knocked under the car so no one could reach it.

Then my boyfriend yelled, "Go get help! I've got him." He had him pinned down.

The intensity of this experience has stayed with me as if it happened yesterday. I can still hear our abductor screaming repeatedly, "I can't wait to squeeze the trigger!" as he fidgeted erratically, waved the gun around, and knocked it up against our heads. And "If you screw up, I'm going to blow your fucking brains out!" It was sheer terror wondering if I was going to see my boyfriend's head blown off and smashed against the windshield at any moment. I recall feeling trapped in the car, looking at the rifle, then at the sidewalk outside. For a few moments my perspective changed and I was on the sidewalk seeing myself in the car. I could feel the cool air on the sidewalk as I looked around. I was free. Then I was back in the car. I later assumed this was an "out of body" experience. This harrowing ordeal changed my life in many ways. As someone once told me, "Once you have found that door to the other side it is easier to find it again." People who have had near death experiences are the same. They've seen and returned from another dimension, so a part of them knows where the door is located. Their connection to the paranormal spirit realm is easier to reach. And things pass through that door for them to see more easily as well.

I also developed an attitude to always try to help people on the spot if they need it. After my boyfriend overpowered our abductor, I dove onto the hood of a car and cried for the man inside to get the police. He took off, so I ran to a well-lit shop in the now darkened strip mall. It was a liquor store. I arrived in shock and drenched by the night's cold rain. I didn't realize until later that I had lost my shoes along the way. Frantic, I begged the attendant for help and to call the police. He announced to the other customers not to go outside, but told me, "I don't want to be involved. There's a phone over there." I was shaking so badly that I couldn't get it together to make the call. So, again, I pleaded for him to just dial them for me. After far too much thought, reluctantly he finally did and shoved the phone to me not saying a word. I got enough words out until the police made the connection who I was. They had been looking for us. We were finally rescued.

What I witnessed in that liquor store was one of the most disgusting sides of human nature. I never want to be that person who doesn't at least try to do something to help another human being. I don't want another person to feel as desperate and alone as I did that night. Sure, maybe I'm not the best at doing organized volunteer work. But, if a situation presents itself where a person or people need help, I will step up and try to do whatever I can. I've learned that "being present" is some of the best help you can offer to someone.

Honesty paid off in that crisis situation as well. Recently, I was reminded of something I wrote when I was about 12. When we were young it was customary to write our names or phrases on the train trestle over a private lake, where we had a house. All the kids on the lake did it. I wrote my name but wasn't sure what else to write. Out of the blue I wrote, "The truth will set you free." For years, driving the boat past that phrase, I always thought how goofy it probably was to write it. No one else wrote anything nearly as profound. But the truth, or my honesty, did literally set us free years later.

In the summers between my college years, I worked in different cities. In Nantucket, Massachusetts, I just showed up and found a job. For my senior year I studied in Venice. After that semester I relocated to Boston.

I worked my way up in various architectural firms until I decided to go back to graduate school in London. Of course, after making this decision, I met a man in Boston who I thought was my future. I still left for London, but returned after a semester to be with him, thinking I could get licensed as an architect by interning for a longer period of time. He was a real estate developer. It all seemed picture perfect with him and with my career doing schools, sports facilities, resorts, and residences, with a major architectural firm. We even had a house with a white picket fence. However, the economy changed and the real estate development market dropped. In addition, Massachusetts changed its architectural licensing law, requiring me to complete my Masters if I wanted to be licensed in the state. I was still content with my job and focusing on our relationship. But my boyfriend was only focused on saving his business. I wasn't a priority at all and he barely spoke with me even though we were living together. Ultimately, we were too young to resolve our issues. I eventually decided to move to Southern California, in 1989, to start over and get my architectural license. I was also tired of the cold weather.

꽁ꗚꗚꗛ

2

SUNNY SOUTHERN CALIFORNIA

ON THE PLANE, going to Los Angeles for a job interview, I met a contractor from Western Australia. When the recession kicked in I did approximately thirteen projects for him around the globe. I've always believed in fated points in your life. And this was one of them.

After working with a few firms in Southern California, I started my own firm as a licensed architect. Although it was a good move, it was also somewhat imposed on me with the recession. I specialized in International Exhibition Design, and Custom Residential.

One day, when I was on an outing with an artist

I had hired for a show in Singapore, he suggested we go and see the taping of a talk show, "Party Crashers." His friend was the host. The guest for the day was a "no-show" so the host asked me if I'd go on the show as an "International Architect." Strangely, I always carried a nice dress and my portfolio in the trunk of my car. I was afraid of something happening to my portfolio so I always kept it with me. And I wanted to always be prepared in case an occasion came up where I needed something nice to wear while I was out in Los Angeles. So, I was prepared, and agreed. Following the airing of the show, I was informed that the executive producers wanted me to co-host the show for more episodes. This was the beginning of my acting career in Los Angeles.

For several years I worked as an actress and model for commercials, television, and feature films such as "Friends," "Everybody Loves Raymond," and "The Crow: City of Angels." As a requirement of SAG (Screen Actors Guild) I had to change my name due to there already being a famous actress named "Mary Martin." So I became Marie Micheaux, another family name. The film business became the focus of my life and architecture became a hobby. I had always been a television and film junkie, so being a part of this world seemed natural and exciting for me. One of my nicknames as a child was "Tube Captain."

I realize, while reading this, it may appear that I just moved smoothly from one thing to the next. Maybe because when you look back on your life you can see how it all fits together. But it was hardly like that. There were some very difficult times for a long time, with little money and little hope. But I allowed myself to be open to new experiences, and things eventually changed.

I also believe that if you are aware of what life is offering, then you notice how life often offers you another chance at some things. Situations tend to repeat themselves. The events may not recur exactly as the previous time, but in a similar way, so that you can make a different choice or develop a different perspective that you didn't see the first time around.

When I was in Los Angeles, I had another encounter with violence slightly similar to the one in Virginia. I was out at a club with a friend named Sally, and we were on our way home. I was driving. We stopped at a Burger King drive-thru on Sunset Drive, the main club strip. It was late at night and the line was long. We were behind a limo that seemed to be taking forever. These ruffian girls behind us were annoyed and sat on their horn and screamed out the window. They were looking for trouble.

The limo in front of us still didn't move and my friend became seriously agitated. Finally, Sally foolishly flipped the girls the bird. This really set them off. They'd found the trouble they were looking for!

They screamed, "We're going to kill you bitches! We're coming after you!" And they continued honking the horn. Now, this wasn't a great section on Sunset Drive. The Burger King was down the road a ways from the glitz and main activity. And we were sandwiched between the limo and them.

When I arrived at the window, I announced to the server, "We have a problem." Of course, you'd have to be in another galaxy not to notice that there was a problem outside with all the commotion. I asked him to have security speak with them and to hold them back so they wouldn't come after us. But, of course, once we passed the drive-thru window the crazy chicks behind us just followed and tried to run us off the road.

"We're going to kill you!" They shouted over and over.

This was LA. People have guns! These girls weren't club-goers. They seemed like gang girls, who were known to be more violent than the guys to prove themselves.

I weaved in and out of traffic trying to get the attention of a police officer. But, of course, there wasn't one when we needed one. My friend shouted at anyone we drove by on the street to call the police. But we were always moving. How could they find us? I didn't know these streets in this area. I feared the crazy chicks could easily steer us down a dead-end street I didn't know and open fire. But suddenly, something seemed familiar. We had circled around and were back at the Burger King. I drove up to the security guard who was now outside and told him to call the cops. He waited beside us for them to arrive. But I knew they could shoot him as well.

Sally cried hysterically and shrieked, "Take off! Drive! We're going to die!"

The adrenaline pumped through my system. I'd already tried to get away and couldn't lose them. There, we were sitting ducks. But maybe the police would arrive in a few more seconds. So I watched, ready to peel out if things escalated, which they did. But now we faced a more difficult situation. There were now more junker cars with guys and girls in them circling the Burger King. They must have called their friends! The Burger King was like an island. How could we ever get out of there now? They would all follow us, or shoot us as we tried to cross their line. And, now, not just one car had unhinged characters screaming that they wanted to kill us. All of the cars did! The poor security guard looked nervous but tried to be tough. I didn't even know if he carried a gun. One car I hadn't seen before sped up and raced through the parking lot near us. I was ready to floor it, but the security guard was in the way. Someone in the car unloaded their drinks and trash on the guard and the car raced back to be in the circle. Was this their warning strike and the next one would be real? Where were the police? I made sure the guard was okay while my heart and mind raced. The seconds seemed like minutes. Sally continued to shout at me to take off. I could feel that something was going to happen if the police didn't show up soon. It was in the air. Maybe I had to do something else. But what? My senses were acute. I could see every car at once. I knew that the next time someone acted I would be forced to react. I would have to trust my instincts on what to do. There was my friend, the security guard, and myself, and I was the one driving the car. So, I just waited for some slight change in movement in our tormentors' pattern. Then, as if the wind shifted, there was movement. And I heard sirens. The troops had arrived! The cars dispersed quickly in all directions.

My gut had told me to try to hold out there for just a little longer for the police and I prayed. But the situation could have gone either way. All you can do is make the best decision you can at the time and go with it.

The police informed us that they were indeed gang members and a police officer had been killed at that Burger King the night before. Then the police escorted us home to make sure we weren't followed.

Of course, we were pretty wound up once we were back. It was a mixed feeling of shock and relief. As the night began to settle, I reviewed the events of the evening in my mind and had the epiphany of experiencing this similar feeling before when I was in Virginia. But, when I was younger, I believed if my boyfriend hadn't been driving the car when we were abducted I would be dead. I didn't think that I could have driven. I always held onto that belief and finally accepted it as truth. It took me a long time to process and accept my weakness. But, this time, I was driving. Maybe I had developed more strength from my past. Or maybe I could have driven before and made the best decision I could at that time. Maybe I wasn't weak at the core, but strong. It was a horrible experience that night, but I found some peace in it. It was confirmation of my belief in determinism vs. randomness. That night had to have been fated.

3

FLORIDA

AT THE END of 1999 I fled California. After a "final straw" I recognized that a six-year relationship I'd had with a man in the music business was unhealthy. So I packed up my life of twelve years in four days, jumped into my convertible Jaguar, and left. I thought the only way I was to have a life and get away from the situation was to have some distance. I relocated to Miami Beach, Florida, and started over. I pretty much only told my family where I was going. I wanted a clean break.

Eight months later, I received an email that I thought was from my ex-boyfriend, wanting me back. But when I opened it, I saw that one of his current girl-friends had broken into his email account, copied every personal letter that went back almost the entire time we were together, and sent out the mass to everyone on his contact list. From reading these emails I found out that he had cheated on me the entire time we were together. He was another Tiger Woods needing several women a day. Once these women realized I had been with him so long, I received hate mail. In LA the situation became volatile when the sleuth herself went nuts. Moving to Miami killed my acting career, but saved my life. It's one thing when a relationship doesn't work out for one reason or other, but to realize someone knowingly manipulated you and wasted your life for years, is hard to reconcile. I kept telling myself, "Sociopaths have no remorse so you can't tell when they are lying." But I still felt stupid.

After much reflection I moved past that disaster, but I never had a boyfriend the entire time I was in Florida. Over the years, I briefly dated a spectrum of possibilities from Princes to lottery winners and everything in between. I became comfortable over time with my own company and I knew that I didn't need a relationship to survive. Of course, I wanted someone to share life with, but only the right one for me.

I focused on my work and interests—my screenwriting and songwriting, real estate investments, and my own building projects, mostly. I also obtained my real estate license, bartended in the famous South Beach, and modeled on the side.

For the first few years we had some active hurricanes. The property taxes and insurance sky-rocketed. This made getting ahead more difficult, but I was determined to get over the hurdles. At one point in the real estate market, I had built up my portfolio to having over two million dollars in equity. I often worked seven days a week and lived on a construction site. It was always, "Just one more project" then I could take time off and only focus on my writing. This thinking was a trap! The workers were the worst I had seen anywhere. The majority were liars, cheaters, and thieves. My "challenging" projects turned masochistic. On one project I had to rebuild the bathroom 11 times! And I was alone. I did the design, the financing, real estate, and general contracting.

At long last, by 2008, things were steady. Life was beautiful. I was still alone, so I decided to have a child by myself. I always wanted to have an incredible husband and children, but "Mr. Right" didn't show up in time. Instead of trapping someone, I decided to be honest and have a child alone, with the hopes that "Mr. Right" would understand if he ever did show up. One of the happiest days of my life was finding out I was pregnant on Christmas Day, after working with a fertility clinic for many months. But my joy was short lived, as life turned with the economy. The banks changed the terms on my loans for no reason, not even allowing me to finish construction. My empire was strategically interconnected so this unexpected maneuver of the banks set up a potential collapsing domino affect with my assets.

People who didn't experience this financial crisis became unnecessarily judgmental on the wrong people as well. Criticism is easy from a distance. All of us who were a part of the real estate investment business generally played by the rules. We didn't do anything wrong. We made decisions based on these "rules" and made our payments as scheduled. The banks changed the rules with little consequences to themselves, and much of the blame spread onto the real estate investment players who were supposedly "in over their heads." But this was not the case in many circumstances, if the banks had performed as promised. The bank representatives also refused to negotiate with you unless you were behind on your payments. They even advised you to stop making payments for at least 4 months. So, even if you wanted and could continue making your payments on time to maintain good credit, they forced you into a dangerous negotiating position that they intended to win. The general public did not see, or understand, this reality.

I was also in a high-risk pregnancy, with doctors gauging me with extra appointments so they could take more money. I thought I was keeping it all together with exercise, sleep, meditation, healthy eating and gaining a whopping fifty pounds, but there was a problem, probably from the stress. The most criminal of all the banks' behavior was when my second mortgage bank telephoned right at the time when I was doubled over in pain, hemorrhaging and frantically trying to reach the doctor. They would not get off the phone even after telling them I was experiencing a medical emergency. I'd hang up but they called back immediately with more harassment from a different phone number. They did this about eight times, tying up my phone line when I desperately needed help. I lost my only child, my son, Jacques.

The next few years I battled grief and the banks. It was like a hurricane had hit my life and I was performing triage to save what I could without losing it all. I did a short-sale on my residence. The bank tortured me for nearly a year on that. I never knew if a marshal would show up at the door from one day to the next to tell me that it was being foreclosed on, or if I would receive a letter that the bank had accepted the short-sale. See, there are separate departments racing against time. There's the foreclosure department, the short-sale department, and the loan modification department. But, as I learned from a friend whose wife was dying of cancer, and who was going for a loan modification, whoever finishes first wins. They foreclosed on him and a week later he received a letter that his loan modification was approved. But his place was gone.

Another major stressor was the law about deficiency in Florida. The banks can come after you for 20 years for any deficiency (loss of money) they feel you owe them from a short-sale or foreclosure, unless they agree to accept the loss. The fear of getting a deficiency judgment was paralyzing, which made this time while working out the short-sale even more stressful.

On the day before my move, I hired some workers to load the truck with the heavy things. They had done a great deal of work for me in the past and I had paid them well with bonuses when I had money. Now I was barely making it. We had just loaded the truck and I was hobbling around with a fractured foot from an accident two weeks prior. Once the last chair was on the truck, the workers blackmailed me for more money than we had originally agreed upon. They said that if I didn't pay them $40 an hour they would take everything back off the truck. It was the end of the day and I had to drive the truck in the morning! I was exhausted and at the end of my rope. My cousin, Alice, who was there for moral support, witnessed the screaming meltdown I had with the workers on the front lawn. I was exhausted and in tears. I really couldn't believe they could be so cruel after I had always treated them so well. I tried to hold firm. I was sick of being lied to and manipulated. The battle went on and on. Finally, I gave them $25 an hour to get rid of them and ordered them off the property. I was revolted by all the greed I had witnessed in those recent years with workers, banks, attorneys, and realtors. I had taken a lot of hits from the opportunists. It's serious work trying to keep other peoples' hands out of your pockets.

That night, Alice and I went out for a peaceful dinner to celebrate. I'd gotten it all done even with a fractured foot. We toasted my new life. I had very little money now, but I didn't have anything hanging over me. I could start over anew. We spoke of how soon I would be living my new life and toasting with Prosecco in Venice. See, the only way I could endure those last years of agony was to continually visualize a positive future. I would look at apartments for rent in Venice for hours on the computer and think, "I can leave this house and have that fabulous apartment. I can let go of my life in Florida and live in my favorite city." With a few things left to sell, I had barely enough to make the move. I would make it work.

Time would eventually heal my grief, anger, and exhaustion. Now, I needed serious rest because I had developed anxiety attacks from stress, particularly while driving. And I needed to feel the joys of life again.

❧❧❧

4

NORTH CAROLINA

ON AUGUST 13, 2011, I left Florida and arrived in North Carolina after a long drive with a good friend. I was emotionally and physically exhausted. I expected to be greeted by family members thrilled that I would be in town for a while, and empathetic to my suffering and offering compassion. I was excited to spend time with them. I was going to stay at a family summer property for a while to rest and finish resolving some financial matters. But what I expected to happen did not. I had not lived in North Carolina since I was 17. They had lives that worked with me at a distance. It was painful to realize that some of the family members didn't want me in town for very long. They weren't there for me when I needed help. I believe they felt that their lifestyles were somehow changed and diminished with my presence, instead of enriched.

Upon my return, I found my aunt, who I was named after, very ill. I focused on helping her and my cousins as much as I could until she passed away. This was devastating for all of us.

As the months sped by the winter was soon upon us. I became a recluse in the cabin. The temperature was reaching below 30 degrees and the place was not heated. I felt like a true mountain woman collecting wood and getting fires burning early to have the house warm by the evening.

Finally, I closed the house for the winter and I made another trip to Miami to work things out with the Italian Embassy. It is not so easy to get an elective residency. The embassy wants to see substantial money in the bank. I would barely make their minimum once another small contract closed, but that wouldn't be for a few more months. So, I decided I'd go to Italy as a tourist and return for my visa once the contract closed.

One enormous mistake I made before leaving Miami was trying to do something for myself by having Botox. I only wanted a little from the referral I had researched. However, the person did not listen to my needs and concerns from past experiences, and gave me too much. My brow dropped so drastically that in the first week I could barely see. The extra skin from my lids hung over my eyes, so I had to lift it with my hand to see. The drooping was creating huge wrinkles where I didn't have them previously. I had blurred vision, headaches, neck aches and lost feeling in my left thumb and wrist. All of these symptoms were possible side effects from the drug.

Leaving North Carolina was bittersweet. I would miss the 5:00 pm happy hours, sitting in the living room with the folks watching the dogs play. I would miss watching movies with my brother, John, and the few outings I had with my mother. I would miss just being with my family. But it was time for me to go. Now I could start to create the life I had envisioned in Venice. I could move onto my next phase, after spending years resolving work issues. I was ecstatic to finally focus on my writing and my music, though it was not in the way that I had originally planned.

5

A LITTLE MORE
ON GHOSTS

THE PARANORMAL HAS become very trendy. People openly discuss ghost sightings, aliens, shadow people, entities, fairies, angels, demons, spirit guides, and other supernatural beings. As for me, I have seen and experienced what I believe to be ghosts, astral projections, and visitations. And I must have angels watching over me.

When I lived in Boston, I woke up once in the night to see an old woman standing over the bed. She looked very tired and sad. She had her hair pulled back in a bun and she was wearing a housedress. Later, I found out she had died in that house.

One time, in my house in Miami, I was having a

party with several people from meditation class. Some were also gifted. The doorbell kept ringing but no one was at the door. They all commented that there were spirits in the house. I made peace with them after one night when one appeared holding his severed head, trying to frighten me. I told him firmly, "I'm not afraid of you! I'm not leaving! You either need to leave or we have to get along in the house." From then on I didn't experience them much, except when having a party. They would make the corks fly out of the wine bottles. I also have a photo of an image of one standing in the kitchen. I believe they did things to protect me if I had someone in the house they didn't like. They would create distractions for me, keeping me from the person. For instance, once the water tank of the toilet spontaneously broke in half, even though it wasn't being used, and began flooding the house. I had to spend the time with the house and not with the person. Soon afterwards, I found out that the person wasn't honest or sincere and I shouldn't have been with him in the first place. These bizarre situations happened a few times with the same result. Perhaps they were mere coincidence, but I don't think so. It became common knowledge with my friends about the house because they saw things there as well. After researching the house, I learned that the original owners wrote Vaudeville shows and were used to having grand parties at the house. That is the likely reason they showed up during parties. And surprisingly, only people connected to the Entertainment Business ever lived there. I sold the house to a film director from Chile.

Astral projections are a little tricky to explain. I didn't know what they were until I had an experience and had to investigate what it was. I had a huge fight with someone I was seeing named André. It had been a few months since we had spoken. One night I heard someone in my room. The noise woke me up. I was too afraid to move. I thought someone had broken in. I lay there quietly, trying to think of what to do. Then I realized it was a "ghost" of André, and that he was sorry. He just kept looking over me, and then he disappeared. The next day, I spoke to everyone I knew about what it could be. I also checked through some friends to see if he was dead. But he was alive.

It was an astral projection. In his conscious state he wouldn't let himself come see me, but in his unconscious state, he did. We did not speak for 5 years. One day, he finally called. For some reason, he couldn't seem to erase my number from his phone, even though he had tried. Accidentally, he called thinking he was calling his mother. We had a good talk. I asked him, "Did you have an intense dream about me that you were in my house a few months after the last time I saw you?"

He replied, shocked, "How did you know that? I didn't tell you." André was not a believer in anything but traditional Christianity. I told him what had happened and it spooked him because the timing was completely accurate. He began believing more that there were things out there we don't fully understand. He knew we had a strange connection. I would often pick up on what he was thinking at the exact time he was thinking it.

On another occasion, I had been speaking with a producer about a metaphysical film I had written. He was also a "sensitive" and had experienced a near death experience after a heart attack. We seemed to have a strange psychic connection. From our many discussions on the phone about spirituality and my screenplay, we developed an intense attraction towards each other although we had not met in person. Then he suddenly disappeared and I didn't hear from him. Weeks later, I saw a ghost of a man on my dresser, doing yoga. He was wearing a blue shirt and pants and looked like he hadn't shaved in a while. Eventually, the producer resurfaced, telephoned, and we discussed my experience. He was remorseful about disappearing, but an old girlfriend had shown up pregnant and claiming he was the father, which sent him into another mode. But he found my experience unusual, because he said he had been wearing similar clothes and doing a lot of yoga in that time. I sent him many photos of my 3-bedroom house. I had been sleeping in the guest room but didn't tell him this. He recognized a room from a vision or dream he had. He described his perspective in the room that would have placed him on the dresser in the guest room. When we finally met I recognized him as the person who had been on the dresser.

"Astral projecting" is also recognized as "remote viewing." From as early as the 1970's, the US government initiated the "Stargate Project" to gather information from psychic means for military purposes. This project was terminated in 1995, claiming not enough valuable information was retrieved. Since then other experiments have been undertaken with mixed results.

Another experience I have encountered on many occasions is what I term "visitations." In a deep dream state I will encounter both living and dead beings. I usually see them in an empty space, where we have a conversation. Sometimes they are people who have passed over, who want me to tell a loved one something. Sometimes I have a conversation with someone who is living, and explaining a situation. When I reconnect with the person when I am awake, the situation we discussed is accurate.

Once, I saw someone in "the space" walking towards me. He scared me. When I awoke, I turned on the television to hopefully disperse the creepy feeling that still lingered. The news was discussing the execution of a murderer that had taken place that night. The photo was the same as the man I'd seen. Previously, I had not been tuned into the news for a while because I was finishing a project.

Another profound situation happened at the Miami Yacht Club. One night, when the security cameras were on and the restaurant was locked up, the television was ripped from the wall. On the video there was a definite man-ghost wearing a cap, pulling the television from the wall. Many of the members recognized him and the cap. He was a fellow member who had passed away that year. It was one of the most clear and amazing videos I have ever seen. But what actually amazes me even more is that there are still people out there who don't believe in this other dimension, even when there are videos to prove its existence.

❧❦❧

6

STARTING OVER
AT THE PALACE

February 13th

THE NATIONAL NEWS didn't penetrate my euphoric bubble while preparing for my trip. When I finally did hear what was going on in the world it was the news of Whitney Houston's death. I heard the report while waiting for my flight at the Asheville Airport. She was one of my favorite entertainers, and her death struck a chord with me because she was my age. The shock weighed heavily on my heart as I watched time pass on the clock on the wall. I couldn't help but reflect on some personal friends who had also died too soon. They had ended a chapter in their life, and then the big "C" came upon them and took them. My theory is that you continually have to visualize a future in order to have one. Obviously, certain situations are fated, but one's mind must play a part in your destiny as well. Just think of all of the older couples who take their last breaths around the same time. I knew Whitney was doing a new movie when she died, but I wondered about her mindset.

Even though we were the same age, my achievements paled in comparison to hers. She was a mega-talented, superstar icon. I was just a mere traveler, journeying from one thing to the next. But I felt good about myself. It was hard to visualize a future in that dark time in Florida. At times I would panic over this. But I focused on what I loved and tried to create an image that was outside the box. The farther I could get away from that lifelong dream of domesticity and motherhood, the better. And now I was taking off to manifest the new future I had designed. I could see a beautiful life ahead of me. For years I had wanted to live in Venice again. Now, instead of thinking about it, I was doing it.

To say I had a terrible flight is an understatement. I had one of the worst seats I had ever experienced on an airplane. The seat was jammed next to the wall without the armrest space. It was so close that I couldn't sit up straight, or my head would hit the ceiling. It amazed me that I had to pay full price for a seat that was obviously Jerry-rigged in that position to pack in more passengers. There was no way that this seat could have passed the minimum space requirements. Someone had to have been paid off somewhere. One could only question what other things in the plane were substandard.

The poor guy on the other side of the plane, in the same position, naturally had the same complaint. But he was about fifty pounds heavier and eight inches taller than I. He wasn't overweight, but there was still no way you could cram him into that seat. So they gave him the last seat available on the flight, which was in the middle. But I was stuck. At least there were some small women in the seats next to me, so I could squeeze some air space out of my neighbor's area. Of course, it was impossible to get any sleep under those conditions. There was a time when flying was considered "fun." Now, a person tolerates the inconveniences and stays focused on the destination.

As the Venice Airport came into sight, I was revived by that young 20 year-old schoolgirl who surfaced with that spark of nervousness and excitement. I was back.

It was a brisk February day. The papers in the States had stated that Venice had turned into an "Ice City." It was about 45 degrees, and not nearly as cold as I had expected. I took the vaporetto (waterbus) across the lagoon and was awed by the natural beauty. The sunlight danced across the chop in the water, as the sea grass spires swayed across the mounds that rose up from the marshes. It was an orchestra conducted by the breath of the spirit of the city. Snow dust still covered some of the higher ground and outer islands, with the snowy white Alps in the distance. After passing Murano, a Venetian island famous for centuries for their glass, the cold north side of the ancient city emerged. The austere façades of perfectly proportioned windows punched into the walls, draped across the sky like a tapestry. We stopped briefly at Fondamenta Nove, an area I knew well. I had traversed that fondamenta many times as a student. My apartment was on the corner of the fondamenta and a canal that overlooked the ornate façade of San Michele, the cemetery island. The views from our top floor kitchen window were permanently etched in my mind. They were paintings of the pink sky at sunrise and sunset, with either San Michele, or the cranes from another part of the city in the foreground. Depending on the time, the images were either highlighted or shadowed against the sky. The kitchen was the most inspirational workplace in the flat. With the long hours from being in architecture, I saw the light at all hours.

We continued on around the city, to the stop at San Stae, with a change to Ca' d'Oro on the Grand Canal. I'm always amazed when traveling around Venice just how large and intricate the city really is. Tourists believe you can see Venice in a day. But to quote a Venetian, "They don't see Venice! They see nothing!" From all the years I've been visiting, Venice still teaches me about its architecture and culture as if I'm in a familiar new city.

Since I had not been to Venice in three to four years, I planned out my arrival in great detail so the trip would go smoothly. I booked a room at the Hotel Pesaro Palace, on the Grand Canal next to the Ca' d'Oro stop. It was a recently renovated, historic boutique hotel designed with a mixture of the modern and Venetian style from the Golden Age. I splurged to stay in this hotel. My mother always cited me as "an enigma" because I could move easily from living with very little as I did on the construction site to living in "a palace."

My room was not the fabulous one from the photo with the view of the Grand Canal, but it was still very opulent on the ground floor, with a garden view. It was bold in red and gold with silk drapes, and fabric on the walls. An exquisite red and clear Venetian chandelier was over the bed that took up much of the room. The headboard of the bed was on the wall that was directly on the alleyway from the boat stop. I was concerned about being disturbed by the heavy traffic and people talking outside. But I figured since I was only there for three nights before I moved into an apartment, I could tolerate it.

I loved the large bath and all the assorted soaps and lotions typical in a luxury hotel. To feel clean and pampered after that nightmare of a flight was a necessity. I had to pee more than usual on the plane which added to my already disgusting feeling. But now I was like a shiny new penny ready to roll into town.

As I ventured down Strada Nova, the wide tourist street of Venice, I came upon a stand with stools around it offering hot sangria. Yes, it was a hot sangria and not Brule, the Venetian hot wine specialty. And to quote a guy at the bar, "It's damn good!" It was a funny little stand, with different fruits displayed like one you'd see in Mexico. A lively and attractive girl, named Letti, served me. And wouldn't you know it, she was from Mexico. She was another captive of Venice. She'd studied there for a while and never left. As the night cooled, I sipped on steaming sangria and watched all the people in outrageous Carnivale costumes pass by. The logistics of getting on some of the get-ups was mind-boggling. Some were multi-layered with lights. I wondered how they fared in the rain…. My mind floated back to Miami Beach for a moment, and being at the Tiki Bar at Monty's, listening to Reggae music. The situations only slightly paralleled each other. But even though I was cold, I was happy I was in Venice.

After a little conversation and a couple of sangrias, I journeyed on to Bacarojazz. This old-time jazz bar had bras hanging from the ceiling that you might not even notice if you didn't look up. At one time they had t-shirts saying, "I left my bra at Bacarojazz." Of course, you had to leave a bra to get the t-shirt. The last time I was there, I left a strapless bra that kept falling down during a date. The t-shirt was a good trade.

When I arrived, I was hoping to meet up with an old friend who worked there, but I was greeted by this sizzling hot, tall, blue-eyed bartender with dark, spiky, fashionable hair instead. The switch to my furnace flipped on. Wow! My whole body was tingling. My romantic life had been shut down, due to my other focuses, for too long. Now I felt like the beast within me had been released. Finally, I could go out and enjoy myself without feeling like the weight of the empire I had built was caving down on me. I was uncaged and unleashed! And, as I saw it, I deserved to have some fun. I deserved a prize, really, for not stroking out through all that stress. I was dizzy from the hormone surge, so I grabbed the bar and carefully seated myself.

"Does Mary still work here?" I asked. Mary was a bartender from New York who had worked there for many years. She had gone back and forth to Venice for years and finally realized she had to commit. Her words had encouraged me to make my leap to the city.

The bartender didn't know her, but had heard of her. He informed me that she left when the new Chinese owner took over a few years back. But her American flag still hung over the bar.

I was relieved he knew some English. I kept getting lost in his words as I stared through those brilliant, blue sparkly eyes. They were as clear as perfect Murano glass beads. And he had a perfect smile and white teeth, not so common in Italy with the smokers. He appeared to be the perfect man, with his lean and elegant features, when he glided around the bar like a Frank Sinatra dance. I couldn't put my finger on why he looked so familiar to me. But wouldn't I remember every detail if I had seen him somewhere before? He seemed too perfect for me not to be replaying our movie of meeting over and over in my head. I would figure it out. But, now, I needed cooling off, so I reached for some long awaited words, "Un Prosecco per favore." And I toasted.

Throughout the evening my eyes stalked Lucio, who finally introduced himself. It was too busy to actually have more of a conversation with him, so I settled in with my favorite dish, sepie nero con polenta, and chatted with other travelers. I met an interesting couple, an engineer and an architect, who lived in Malta. Another couple was visiting from Belgium. I had more interesting conversations outside of my family than I'd had in years. It reconfirmed my decision to move there. As the jetlag slowly set in, I made it an early night and went back to the hotel after dinner. Sleep completely took me over, even with the people walking and talking on the other side of the wall.

❧❦❧

7

WHERE'S MY VALENTINE?

MY BODY THROBBED in a peaceful way as I awoke from a long night's sleep. I was still wiped out physically from the trip, but I was well rested. Today was Valentine's Day. I planned to meet the tall and lean Giovanni that evening. Giovanni was a Venetian charter yacht captain, who had lived in Florida at one time. I met him, the last time I was in Venice, through friends and saw him my last night before going back to the States. I didn't think it would be years before I saw him again, but that was how life played out. I had made the decision to have a child by myself and he was very supportive from a distance. He didn't want children, so it seemed logical to keep him away, though he offered to visit. And time and years danced on. The more I reflected on our time together, I remembered other "red flags." One concerned money. I couldn't tell if he was cheap, or a loyal Venetian only wanting to visit Venetian establishments. But these establishments also offered the "Venetian discounts." He was obsessed with only visiting one of these places to the point of being embarrassing. Another red flag I tried to block out of my memory was from one night when he brought me home and came in for just a few minutes. I went to the restroom and returned to find him with his pants to his knees, underwear up, standing and looking at me as if he had been caught peeing in the living room. I calmly looked him over, and said firmly, "Pull your pants up." Unfortunately, I had learned to deal with bizarre displays of that sort from living in Miami with the Cuban men. No telling what he was thinking or doing. Maybe he'd had too much to drink. I didn't want to believe he was just a wanker. He knew I wasn't the kind of woman to have a romp without knowing him better. I had told him this. I'm not exactly sure what disappointed me more though, his behavior or his skinny ass. Overall, he was classically handsome with refined features. He was more supportive when I was in Miami than some friends who lived there. And he kept in touch with me through all those awful years. At any rate, I felt like when I saw him again we would sort out those red flags one way or another.

We corresponded about my return. I, as the great

romantic, thought that the perfect place to meet was the Hotel Danieli. The Byzantine Gothic palatial hotel had housed four Doges in its history and was built in the 14th century. Upon entering there is a four-storied courtyard with a grand staircase and arches, and balconies that take your breath away. The large marble columns, and rose and cream colored marble floor, scream of elegance. I had everything planned for the evening. I had purchased my favorite bath products, so I felt like a star. I had my hair curled, and I was wearing some new clothes from Christmas with my long white leather and fur coat. I was ready and excited to see him. I also thought having a drink there—a five star hotel—might sort out one red flag. He called and cancelled, saying he was sick…. I was disappointed, but I had a plan. I contacted Thomas, another person I had dated a few times in the past, who was eager to see me again. We had also spoken that day.

I sat at the bar waiting for Thomas, feeling as special as my surroundings. Then the phone rang. Thomas lived far away and felt like it was too cold outside to travel. He asked to reschedule. Okay, that's two down so far! I still enjoyed my Prosecco at the Danieli. The handsome bartender told me he'd be my Valentine if the evening didn't improve. But I was fine. I actually couldn't remember the last time that I'd had a good Valentine's Day with someone, anyway. I was sitting in this stunning hotel, sipping Prosecco, watching the people in costume and feeling like I was in an interactive theatre production. I liked my own company. I looked and felt fabulous. I was content. That was enough. As the evening arrived, I realized I needed to make dinner arrangements. I told my back-up Valentine I was going to leave and might be back later, on my way home.

After a quick bite out, I ventured to Al Remer, a dark and cozy romantic pub on the Grand Canal that overlooked the Rialto Market. This was where I first met Giovanni. The owner, a British woman, tastefully decorated the rustic and exposed beam structure with wrought iron sconces and candles throughout. The dark wooden tables and impressive stone bar also contributed to the warmth of the place. It was casual but elegant. Romance was destined to surface amidst all the candlelight that night. I decided I was going to just have a good time with no expectations. It was Valentine's Day. I looked fabulous and I was going to have a great time. I hadn't just cut loose and had fun for fun's sake in a long while. There was an awesome band playing. And the bar staff were hot at this venue. They all looked as though they had walked off a page of GQ.

As I ordered a Prosecco, a quirkily attractive bald-headed man approached me. At that point in my life, bald was beautiful. Interesting was beautiful. After having a boyfriend who I would spend five hours a shot fixing his dreadlocks, bald was indeed a positive quality. Sergio was a police officer from San Remo, one of my favorite little hideouts. As the music blasted it became more difficult to talk, so we danced. We danced and danced and danced. He was an exceptional dance partner. I loved being in the arms of such a strong man. It was comforting to feel cared for, even if only for the duration of a song. The music brought everyone together in the place. Many of us were strangers, but we all began conversations with one another. A group invited us to join them at their table. Many spoke English and shared all kinds of tales. I felt like I fit in there. Sergio was the perfect companion, being warm and attentive. Our table became the sun with everyone revolving around it. I was introduced to so many interesting and new people from someone at the table, who knew someone who knew someone else. It was difficult to keep all the stories and names straight. A few women returned from disastrous Valentine's Day events. One was in tears. I was on the two down and one to go scenario, but I was having a great night. I wasn't concerned how things would end up with Sergio. I was enjoying the moment. Self-confidence is a highly attractive aura. Even if, in reality, I didn't feel so terrific with my added weight and the fallen face, I did the best with what I had and was loving life. I didn't put pressure on myself to be perfect, or care what anyone thought. I was just appreciating my new freedom and I was ecstatically happy. I even met a potential singer for some of my music. It was incredible how this attitude attracted so many people. It was different from Miami, where you're just a piece of meat. And, if you're not looking like a 20 year-old model, you have no use. People acted sincerely interested in who I was and what I was doing.

The evening came to a close as the band stopped playing. Sergio politely offered to walk me back to the hotel. It's amazing how sobering a walk of a mile or so can be in the icy cold after a warm night like that. When we arrived at the hotel I could tell he was intimidated. The entrance to the palace was through an ornate wrought iron gate into a private garden. It screamed "Money," although I had a deal. So now was the defining moment of the night. I looked into his eager, curious face, and he kissed me. But there was nothing. Not what I had expected at all. I thought there would be sparks, or at least one spark. But nothing. "Thank you for the evening." I said. I looked briefly again at him. He nodded and I turned and walked alone through the gate, knowing I wouldn't be likely to see him again. Three down for the count of the night, but it was an extraordinary Valentine's Day.

8

THE NEW FLAT

FTER A SLOW day and night to recover from Valentine's Day, my three nights at the palace had ended. On February 16th I moved my bags across the Cannaregio zone of Venice to the Castello zone. Of course, I did it in a few trips, having to maneuver over about six bridges. I was renting an apartment temporarily, from an acquaintance I had rented from before. This place was much smaller than the other flat I had rented—only about 430 square feet. It was located in a corner building on the first floor (the second floor in the US). For a small space it was laid out very well, with one bedroom and a combined living room/ kitchen, and windows all around. The windows faced the narrow calli (alleys), but there was light that streamed in. The calli were charming with bakeries, shoe shops, restaurants, and other artistic signs and light posts that framed the view. There was also a vegetable market nearby. I had stayed near that area before.

Thomas stopped by after I made a desperate call to him to turn on the heat for me. It was getting pretty cold as the evening was setting in. All the appliances in Italy were tricky and I didn't want to misinterpret the Italian words on them, particularly the gas ones. Thankfully, he came to my rescue. It was nice to be reunited with him. I had known him now for about six years. We met in a glass shop where he worked. I had seen him on two previous trips to Venice. He had a very expressive face with large, round soulful brown eyes. It seemed easy to read his thoughts through those portals.

He was surprised I would stay in a place so small. Even though I mentioned my financial situation had changed in recent years, this didn't register with him. We actually never discussed money in earlier years, but he assumed I had it from seeing my traveling. So, I calmly explained my situation again to him. It's amazing how people's attitudes towards you can change when your finances change.

He killed our warm reunion moment when he blurted out in a judgmental tone "I don't understand how you can have so much and lose so much!"

Of course, that "You're stupid!" look was plastered all over his face. He didn't need to even say it. Sadly, I'd seen that look before. And yes, how can you not be in my situation without feeling like you screwed up somehow? How could I have such extreme reverses? Why couldn't I have saved more? But, like the others who had made the same comments, he had always worked a normal job. He didn't know real estate, property taxes, insurance, health costs, etc., in the US. He had never owned his own home, but stayed with his rich girlfriend from time to time, who he always talked of leaving. He hadn't really taken any life risks. It takes courage to go for what you believe in. As someone once told me, "People look at the score in the end, not what happened in all the innings." I just had to look at my losses as a bad inning and not the end of the game.

Still, it's a horrible feeling when someone, particularly a friend, gives you that "look" and offers condescending advice, even when you know it's out of ignorance. On some level, I knew it was so he had the upper hand over me also. People, by nature, tend to do that. But it was just another area where I had to accept the consequences of my choices. And, as the saying goes, "Better to have loved and lost than never to have loved at all." That was how I felt about my dreams. I had gone for them.

He connected me with a guy named Tino, about a larger flat that was in his same building, later that night. It was more than I could afford. I never saw Thomas after that. He was always "busy." Of course, I also blamed his absence on my new look. I must have appeared fat and stupid to him. But I guess I was fortunate to see his true character. I knew I needed to meet people who appreciated me for the woman I was now, and who understood my experience. There were people out there. I had met a few of them already.

🙐🙐

9

PARTY HEARTY

I BELIEVE THE NOISE started in the flat as soon as I moved in. I heard people partying until 3:00 am most nights, talking, laughing, and trying to over talk the next person. I figured they were walking back from someplace. In the mornings I woke to the sound of carts on the alley and more talking. It was a loud banging noise like wood against the stones. It seemed strange because the carts I had seen always had rubber wheels. Still, somehow, I figured it was the trash people or the vegetable stand around the corner setting up. But it was so early—5:30 am—that I never got to see them pass by, since they woke me with their yammering. It always sounded like they were under or near my bedroom window. The small flat was charming, reasonably priced, and near Piazza San Marco. I considered just staying there, but I couldn't take the noise. The echoes along the calli, and piercing melodic accents, grated on my nerves and literally pained my sensitive ears. I would close up the wooden shutters, which helped with the noise, but that didn't block it completely. It created a different kind of hollow sound. Sometimes I would open the windows and tell people on the street to be quiet. Sometimes they were there, sometimes not. I assumed they were around the corner just out of sight.

I had some good contacts to find another flat. So I just kept looking. I saw about five places. I considered taking one in the middle of March, once some money I was expecting came in.

My days were like living in famous paintings. I visited the Rialto Market—an 11th century landmark—near the Grand Canal and the Rialto Bridge. Tables were lined up and filled with perfectly laid out fresh fruits, vegetables, and fish. It was an artistic education viewing so many different types of sea creatures beautifully displayed across the ice. Being part of such an historic custom transcended the basic life experience of just going to the market.

One day, while I was walking along the fondamenta near the Doges Palace by Piazza San Marco, I turned to see the light over the church of San Giorgio across the lagoon. The gondolas were nestled to the side. This feeling of awe swept over me like some mystical wave. I just stood there, feeling emotional and almost powerless. I couldn't believe I was part of something so awesome. I couldn't believe that I actually ended up in a place of such greatness.

I was extremely happy and optimistic, though getting increasingly more tired from the late night partiers. I even asked someone on the street in the area about the noise. The person didn't know what I was talking about. He dismissed it as Carnevale revelers and concluded that it would stop in a few weeks.

Some nights, my anxiety attacks would creep up, contributing to my insomnia. Between the noise and the anxiety, I couldn't sleep much until 3:00 am. Sometimes I would drift off earlier, but a loud voice would usually wake me. Sometimes it sounded like someone was calling my name, Mary or Marie, very sharply. Sometimes I would hear Mary Martin. But I wrote it off to Carnevale and the fact that there were many people with the name variation of Mary, Marie, and Maria. And many words sound similar in different languages. On the nights when it rained I slept fairly well. Maybe people stayed inside. Maybe the rhythm of the rain, like the sound of the crickets in North Carolina, was putting me in a trancelike sleep. I once read that scientists used different sound rhythms on psychics to help put them into a deep altered state of consciousness, so that they could receive more information. I believe the rain did this for me. At least it put me to sleep.

❧❦❧

10

MAGIC

STARTED RECEIVING THE music I recorded in Nashville by email. The feeling of finally hearing songs I had written, professionally arranged and recorded, was the true manifestation of a dream. I don't even have words for the feelings. Although I played the guitar in my youth and wrote simple songs, my lyrics over the years just collected like lost singles in a singles bar waiting for their other half. I could see their potential but I couldn't find their other half, or someone who could complete the song. For years I looked. In LA I had so many promises of this perfect union, but no one could go the distance. It all was just frivolous talk that never amounted to anything after months or years. The first part of the song might get done, but the musician would lose interest or get involved with other projects and never finished. Then I'd have to start the search over again. I spent decades trying to plug my lyrics. I approached each songwriting possibility with the most positive expectations even after so many years, like a puppy spinning around eager to see his master as if it's the first time. Finally, at 49 years old, I located a group in Nashville, Tennessee, who helped me with my songs and actually completed the music and the recording.

The first song they completed was one I'd written about one of the most devastating times in my life, when I lost my son. I finished writing it on what would have been his birthday. Somehow, that was my tribute to him, although the song dealt with several concepts, one being—"Maybe next time you should ask yourself, would you be different if you knew, what another person has already gone through." People can be selfishly reckless with words and actions, which can greatly affect another person's wellbeing without even knowing the person. It was a concept for developing more awareness with your fellow man. It had been three years since I lost him. But it is something you never forget, although those around you generally do. The song cemented his existence into reality, along with the love I had for him. It was a difficult song to hear, but also healing–as it reaffirmed the strength I had within myself at the time from this love. Somehow, love was triumphant in bringing me back.

Another completed song arrived. Strategically, I had previously dropped by Bacarojazz one night and asked if I could play some of my songs so I could hear how they sounded on their professional sound system. Lucio agreed, but wanted me to stop by as soon as they opened because no one would be there. I could blast the music as loud as I liked.

I arrived as soon as the doors opened. Seeing Lucio was the perfect start of my day. I settled in and gave him a CD to play. It was exhilarating having Lucio and my music together. It was noon, so I ordered a Spritz, a light Italian beverage with Aperol, so I wasn't taking up his time and not ordering anything. Lucio seemed sincerely impressed and supportive of my music as he played it over and over. He opened the doors of the place so the passersby on the street could hear as well. I would work and edit what needed changing. But this was the best work. We would chat and I would watch how elegantly he moved. He was the perfect specimen for a man. He was studying computers, so we discussed the book I was reading about Steve Jobs. I enjoyed his conversation and viewpoints. He was extremely smart and funny, as well as good-looking. I still couldn't place him as I reached deep within to remember why it was that he was so familiar. My gaze obviously made him nervous, because he made a point to bring up his age of 25. But, for me, 25 wasn't a problem. I had briefly gone out with men younger than that. Although he didn't know my age exactly, his hints made it clear that he didn't see me in a romantic way, although he did flirt. But he concluded with a comment on having a girlfriend, so I would know the boundaries. It was humorous seeing how nervous I was obviously making him. He was one of these well-mannered shy Italian guys, making him even more attractive. I continued with the conversation, not bothered by the girlfriend comment. I sincerely just enjoyed his company. His wisdom was similar to mine, particularly before I became jaded from life beating on me. His honesty and purity was refreshing. I left, that day, on a good note with him. I was beaming and the door was open for me to return with more music.

Another day, I returned in the usual way to edit some music. The day seemed more full of energy. Our connection was somehow closer. I was on fire as I stared him down. Our interaction was like a song, or a dance. He began telling me a story of what was going on in his life. I was staring into those sparkly eyes like a crystal ball as he spoke. And it hit me.

"Oh my God!" I blurted out.

Lucio just looked at me, wondering about my over-reaction to his story. I scrambled to try to cover what I was really thinking. But I now knew our cosmic connection. I knew why he seemed so familiar and why I was so comfortable in his company. I knew why I yearned to stop by and see him. I had the answer. Of the thousands of people I reviewed for many months when looking for a sperm donor, he was almost identical to the one I had chosen. The only difference was that my donor was British, while he was Italian. But they looked almost identical. I had only seen my donor from photos, but I would visualize his mannerisms, his movements, and how our son was going to turn out. He had the attributes of how I visualized my son as well. The donor was even a similar age to Lucio. So, he was indeed the perfect specimen of a man! It was as if my thoughts had materialized this person in front of me. I continued trying to follow Lucio's story, but the situation was so remarkable, it was difficult to comprehend the magnitude of this revelation. I couldn't focus. My mind switched back and forth from the ideas of the perfect man and my son. It was as if he was both of them at the same time in my mind and my heart. It was the energy I had envisioned. Then I considered how twisted my attraction for him was. But he actually wasn't either one of those people. My emotions were so conflicted. I couldn't wrap my head around it.

People started streaming in, so I knew it was time to make my exit. I needed logic, or a theory about it all. As I journeyed back to the flat, I focused on what was real. He had become a nice friend. It was healing being in his company. Now I understood one of the reasons why. And on the supernatural level, somehow this man had entered my life. Some force had connected us. It was like there was some cosmic correction to restore balance. What was lost was now found. I was eager to see how it all played out. But I was also just happy to bask in the glow of our budding friendship. That energy was positive. Although it was confusing, the one thing I knew was that I could never tell him. Well, at least not for a very long time.

∾∾∾

11

MY EVOLVING LIFE

EDITED MY MUSIC in the days, as well as researched ideas for a new script or book. Of course, the title "The Donor," was a possibility. Another concept centered on an offer I made to the owner of Al Remer. Her ex-boyfriend had stolen a great deal of money from her and opened his own club. I offered to go undercover for her as a wealthy American investor, to scout out what was going on in the new place. The premise wouldn't be identical but had the concept of dueling clubs in Venice. Somehow, I needed to reinvent myself again and at the same time fully process all my losses. I even considered starting a tour company. At some point in the not so distant future I needed to have an income. Real estate didn't seem so profitable anymore and I was burned out from it anyway.

Getting a life set up in another country wasn't easy. Just organizing a phone and having Internet was a challenge. But, I finally sorted it out and used my Magic Jack to speak for free to the US. I spent my days hopeful, exploring, working on my writing, and having a few crazy nights at Al Remer or Bacarojazz. I continued meeting interesting people and potential singers for my music. There weren't many television shows I could understand, because the Italian was spoken too fast. But there was one show I watched in English called "Disaster Date." Actually, it was a mean-spirited reality show about a person who would set up their friend on a blind date. At the restaurant where the blind date would occur, everyone at the restaurant was actually an actor in on the stunt. The date would go horribly wrong, a huge scene would occur, and the poor "friend" would be totally embarrassed. Then it would be revealed that the "Disaster Date" was a setup. It amazed me how these reality shows were becoming more and more popular, even though they promoted cruelty by embarrassing people. I often thought "Poor sucker," though ironically, some of the dates seemed similar to some of mine in real life.

The late night partying around my flat was getting worse. There were a number of British people whose voices I was beginning to recognize night after night.

They would say terrible things about other people. They would gossip about a person's clothes, how someone was going around behind someone else's back, and basically whether or not they liked certain people. It was vicious talk that made me sick to my stomach. One evening, I heard them speaking about some music they had heard that I felt was from a club nearby. They argued and laughed over the performer. They analyzed it for nearly an hour and argued about whether or not they would actually spend the money on the CD. Criticism of an artist is easy from afar, particularly if you aren't one. The people made me ill.

❧❦❧

12

GOTTA HAVE MY HEELS

EVERY FEW NIGHTS I would go out for an adventure. It was Carnevale and a good time to check out the local musical talent for my own projects. Besides, staying in was not so restful with the noise around the flat. One night I was full of energy, so I got glammed up with high heels and headed back to Al Remer. This pub was one of the few places that actually had live music every night.

On my way over I recited my mantra, "I am the man magnet," over and over, which was my process for going into a crowd where I might not know anyone. Somehow I needed to pull out my best self and self-confidence for the job, because my natural state was being shy and reserved.

Upon my arrival, I was greeted enthusiastically by

all the beautiful boys at the bar. This was a good start for the evening. Then a chipper little woman popped over like an excited little Chihuahua, claiming she had met me on Valentine's Day. Trish was a plain looking blonde with wire-rimmed glasses that took over her tiny face. Except for her perkiness, she had the classic librarian look. She was eager to make new friends and plan things. I was pleasant and tried to raise my energy level to be at least an octave below hers, but I didn't recognize her. I had met so many people that night. I did recall a little of her story being from New York and working with travel magazines primarily as a graphic artist. Though it seemed there was more to the story. I was obviously distracted at the time, but I remembered some holes in her explanation that I wrote off as being "bar talk."

Trish seemed particularly intrigued with meeting me. She introduced me to the host and motioned that we needed drinks, showing she had clout at that restaurant and her drinks were comped. She was very good with conversation and getting to the heart of people. I remember telling her some stories of my past relationships and why I had moved to Venice. I wanted people in my life I could count on to help me if necessary. That's important. I told her the story of how I had fallen in my house in Miami Beach when I tripped on the carpet in my high-heeled shoes. I cut my head open and called a supposed friend for help who ignored my situation. He was busy. As you get older you realize how important it is to have a support system. She also exchanged some personal information, a little "quid pro quo." I've often been too open with personal information. I forget that some people take information to use against you at a later time.

I danced and danced until my feet were killing me. Even if I didn't have a partner, I loved to just get out there and go with the rhythm of the night. By the end of the evening I was worried about how I was going to make it home over all the bridges in those shoes. It was too cold to take them off. Trish suggested she and her friend, the host, escort me back to my flat. It wasn't out of their way. It was common to help women over the bridges in their heels. One evening, a few nights before, I had met a soldier, and his girlfriend wearing very high heels. I linked arms with her and helped him escort her to their destination. You learn to carry an extra pair of shoes with you after being stuck a few times.

It was a pleasant walk back with my new friends. I was thankful when they lifted me over the bridges and helped me along when my legs couldn't take anymore. If you didn't know the customs in Venice, you would think that I was almost passed out from having too much to drink and they were carrying me home, but that wasn't the case.

Trish invited me to meet up the next night at a group dinner. I was ecstatic with all the attention as I thanked them for the evening. I took off my shoes and proceeded up my staircase totally exhausted. My legs throbbed as I pulled myself up by the railing, arm over arm. I had to cancel the next day. I was too tired. I also had appointments to see more apartments the following day.

❧❦❧

13

CAN I DO THIS?

RAFAELA'S FLAT WAS a layout and style I was comfortable with. It was filled with antiques, had a piano in the den, and was twice the size of the little one where I was currently staying. I was concerned about the noise from being on the first floor, although most of the place looked out over a private garden. In general, it suited my needs and I could move in by mid-March. But, as I thought about it, fear struck. What if the people didn't follow through with the closing of my final contract and I didn't receive the money from it in mid-March as promised? I had experienced so much with the banks not following through with the terms of a contract that the concept of a "binding" contract was not a definite thing for me. With Rafaela's flat I needed substantial money up front.

The realtor also made twice as much as they do in the States. Could I risk making a commitment and then losing more money if the deal didn't go through because the money from the contract didn't show up? I certainly didn't need to put more stress on myself. I decided to keep the place in mind and see if it worked out with the arrival of my money. I would also try to have back-ups in case it was rented suddenly. I had no choice but to stay in my current apartment until I knew for sure that money was wired to my account. It was a difficult decision, but hopefully I would only have to wait a few more weeks. Unfortunately, the noise was escalating and not diminishing. Carnevale was over, but the late night partiers still partied on.

 14

ROLLIN'

TRISH WAS QUITE the socializer. Through one of her friends, I was invited to a gallery opening at Giardini, the public gardens. Her friend was an eccentric looking man with bright yellow-rimmed glasses, who owned the gallery but was also a psychiatrist. I found it interesting how his career overlapped his interest in artists and their imagination. The gallery opened onto a picturesque canal, where everyone hung out with a glass of wine. It was a small local gathering, but still full of class and interesting people.

Afterwards, she invited me to join her at a bar on Via Garibaldi, with friends. The commercial part of Via Garibaldi was a very wide pedestrian street cluttered with local shops and cafes. It held a different kind of charm than the glamour around San Marco, particularly in the evening. Even the food was geared toward the local palate.

I received much more attention than expected. Trish seemed to fade into the background. I wasn't sure if it was intentional, or if she was annoyed by it. She was used to being the center of attention, which seemed odd to me. Not her desire, but that so many people actually swarmed around her. Why? Yes, she was friendly, but what made her so special? I liked her but I didn't get it. I had seen this many times in life. A person is arbitrarily selected by a group to put up on a pedestal, with no real foundation for the appointment.

More and more people asked me about my acting experience. One person even brought up a film she recognized me from. This was unbelievable to me because I had done so much obscure work. I looked so entirely different than I did in my acting days, which were 11 years before then. Of course, it was flattering, but hard to believe. Then, to my surprise, I met several people at the table who were also actors. It seemed unusual that Trish knew so many people in the entertainment business, when I believed she had done advertising in New York in the travel sector and not entertainment.

A little girl came to the table, who looked Indian. I was told privately that she had been adopted but was having some difficulties feeling connected to her Caucasian parents. I knew this was an opportunity to help the little girl. I told her my views on adoption, and how cool it was that you can choose your own destiny without any preconceived ideas of how you're supposed to be. You can accept the family qualities you like and not accept the one's you don't. The little girl was happy and excited to hear I was also adopted. She saw herself in a different light, where she was unique and special, and not just different from her peers. Her smile beamed as she left the table, so happy to be chosen by her parents.

The group dispersed, so Trish and I decided to venture back to Al Remer for more live music. She was quiet. It was a long walk so I invited her for a drink at the Danieli on the way over, but she declined in a very snappy way. I just blew it off because I didn't know what had transpired to put her in that mood. After we reached Al Remer, she made it clear she was staying with the host and would not be accompanying me back. I was fine with walking home alone. I actually did not expect her to walk me. I was used to being alone and I'd brought another pair of shoes this time.

The next morning, I was awakened by hearing the name Mary or Marie called out again. It was about 5:00 am.

Then a woman with a British accent continued, "Mary! Mary!"

There was a long pause.

"Mary, I am sorry to have to tell you but I saw (blurred) out last night again with (blurred). I'm sorry to have to tell you this but (blurred) is cheating on you."

"I know … but thank you for telling me," Mary replied.

Then a man joined them who spoke English but with an Italian accent. "Mary–"

Mary interrupted and screamed, "I don't want to speak with you! We're over! You're a horrible person! We're over. I know about (blurred)!"

"It's not what you think!"

"It is what I think. You're a liar! I don't want anything more to do with you!"

"But Mary, Mary, I can explain!"

"Get out of my sight!"

Then it seemed like Mary walked away because the man just screamed in a painful moan. "Mary! Mary! Mary!" Sounding like the scene from "A Streetcar Named Desire" with Marlon Brando shouting "Stella! Stella!"

After it quieted for a minute I cracked the shutters to see who was out there. But it was silent. No one was there. I figured everyone went around the corner to the vegetable stand. I was now wide awake and couldn't go back to sleep. But I had some clarity about my situation. All the times I would hear my name and be awakened was because someone was having a love affair on the other side of the wall. My name is Mary or Marie and I'm living my own life on this side of the wall, while on the other side, only a foot away, another Mary or Marie was living a completely different life. How astounding! Even though sometimes I thought I heard "Mary Martin" the voices were not always clear, so I was likely wrong. I could only ponder the philosophical implications of this bizarre coincidence. We never saw or knew each other, but we were living different parallel lives. I wrote to Trish and my father about the coincidence. I also mentioned to Trish how much the noise in the flat was continuing to bother me.

I stayed in and rested, and did some work that day. I also lined up a date with Giovanni. I was excited, but I sensed it wouldn't go well. There had been too many stories of him having the flu for over a month. The stories didn't add up particularly since I was to see him before playing soccer. I had not seen him in three years so I had no expectations, but I felt like all the bad communication from our supposedly trying to connect was dooming the situation.

15

THE MARILYN WITHIN

HE PLAN WAS to meet Giovanni at the top of the Rialto Bridge. It was a romantic meeting spot with the picturesque view of all the twinkling lights down the Grand Canal. I was feeling self-conscious, knowing he would be seeing a completely different person from before. Thomas was in the same position and that meeting didn't go well. I knew it was vain, but I wanted people to see me looking spectacular after weathering such tremendous hardships. I did my best with what I had and played up my platinum blonde hair that resembled Marilyn Monroe. Men are visual, so I needed to focus on my best assets at that point. I wore red, high heels, one of my furs, and bright red lipstick. I figured I'd channel the Marilyn within to get me through my insecurities. I believe everyone has a little bit of Marilyn within them.

I stopped off on the way at Al Remer, for a Prosecco. All the staff commented on how great I looked and asked the occasion. I told them optimistically that I had a hot date. It was comforting to be amongst a group that was so supportive. They joked and chatted with me while wishing me luck. I became more and more excited by the prospect of reuniting with Giovanni. Even with the red flags, I remembered the good moments, our laughing, him escorting me through the dark calli to all the hidden spots in Venice, and the way he'd look at me so longingly with his hazel eyes.

I arrived at the Rialto Bridge before he did. I scouted from one side to the other taking in the view. Other lovers hugged and kissed against the wall overlooking the canal. I could only fantasize how my evening was going to unfold. The frosty air was just beginning to numb my face and lips, so I knew my first words to him would be a struggle. I hated to wait. Too many thoughts whirled through my head, heightening the anxiety of the moment. Then I saw him round a corner at the bottom of the bridge, and he looked up. I waved and smiled and he acknowledged he saw me. He trotted quickly up the steps to meet me. As he got closer, I noticed he hadn't changed much over the last few years. Time had stood still for him. We shared a long embrace and gazed into each other's eyes. Then he stepped back a few steps to make his point.

"I'm sorry, I only have 30 minutes. I go to play football."

I tried my best to conceal my shock and disappointment. He was giving me 30 minutes of his time after not seeing me for 3 years, when I had spent so much time and energy preparing to see him. At the very least, it was rude. He didn't invite me to the game but wanted me to accompany him to the train station that was about a mile away, leaving me to walk back alone. I paused in disbelief, trying to compose myself. I needed to show some class even though he obviously had none.

"È difficile perché le scarpe," I said, showing him my heels, even though I had flats hidden in another bag. "Maybe we could have a quick drink out of the cold somewhere near here, and then you can go."

"Sì, okay," he replied. He stood, thinking hard as he looked into the sky. "I know. It's near."

I grabbed his arm as he escorted me down the Rialto steps to an area where there were several cozy restaurants and bars."

"Where?" I asked with a smile as I looked over all of them.

"We go … near," he replied with a plan written all over his face and he started walking in a different direction. He walked quickly, so I did my best to keep up with him in those shoes. After almost jogging for about 15 minutes, I realized we were going in the direction of the train station. He had maintained his plan with no regard for me.

"Are we near? I'm sorry but my feet hurt," I said.

"Sì, sì, è vicino."

I stumbled but clung onto his arm. "Dove?" I asked.

He looked around and nodded at a place. "We go here."

We entered a crowded local spot with many young people. It was obviously a cheapo joint. He ordered two "ombre" which was about a shot glass of local wine. There was no place to sit so he expected me to stand, being crushed up against people.

"Could we sit somewhere?"

He looked around and added, "Outside."

We stepped outside and he pointed at a stool against the wall. He motioned for me to sit, and then he proceeded to light a cigarette, standing next to me. He didn't even ask if I minded. It was frigid cold, but I knew we weren't staying long.

"I didn't know you smoked," I said, remembering how we had discussed his not smoking before.

"Sì, I smoke."

I asked him how his apartment turned out. When I last saw him he told me he'd bought a new place that he was "in the process" of renovating. He led me to believe that it was nearly finished and there were workers there every day, and he had to live with his parents just during the renovation. Now he mentioned that he never renovated the place, he had spent his money travelling, and he was still living with his parents. My eyes opened wide in disbelief. I looked at him and saw a different person than I had known. Something was wrong with him.

He added, "Maybe it's something you would like to buy." He continued with an explanation about it.

I listened politely to his description of a shell of a place as my brain was clicking away, adding things up. He knew I was in construction. And BAM! It hit me. He must have been looking for a free ride before. He must have thought I was a wealthy American sucker. I recalled his suggestion of us getting a large place together. I remembered thinking how premature the conversation was. Anyway, I informed him that I was only interested in renting and I was not in the position to buy at the moment. He looked disappointed, but I felt relieved. I saw that final red flag!

Once that small piece of conversation ended,

Giovanni looked at his watch and exclaimed with no hesitation, "I've got to go. Sorry."

"Okay, thank you," I said smoothly as I sipped on my last bit of wine. He nodded nervously, hugged me, and ran off abruptly, leaving me on the porch of a bar somewhere I had never been to.

"Wow." I breathed in and shook my head. I watched as he just got out of sight. It was barely 30 minutes after seeing him. I had mixed feelings. I always knew something was off with him. But he was helpful through some devastating times and I thought we were at least friends. The reality was much different than what was sold to me. I had seen that too many times before. It was a cold, somber long walk back to Al Remer. I was in shock. I didn't even remember to put on my other shoes.

The gang acted surprised to see me so soon, but knew immediately that it didn't go well by the look on my face. I sat quietly on an empty bar stool in the corner and was immediately presented with a large glass of Prosecco. At least now I felt surrounded by friends. I began to get warm again in the golden glow of the candlelight. Everything was going to be all right.

Strangeness was in the air. I had a conversation with someone who explained the story of the building and the stair outside. Centuries ago, I was told, a man cut the head off his wife for infidelity, at the top of the outside stair. I could visualize how the head and the body would have rolled down the stair. Out of remorse he carried the head around, asking for forgiveness. But no one, including the pope, granted him forgiveness. So, he returned to Venice and killed himself after throwing the head in the canal. Evidently, you can see the man and the head rising from the Grand Canal some nights. I thought back on all the history of Venice. So much passion was trapped in the maze of walls. There must be ghosts lurking about everywhere.

I pondered the story while staring at my Prosecco bubbles and the flickering lights, and two guys called and motioned to me from a nearby table. One was a dark, handsome, swarthy type with fairly long wavy hair. He was the kind of guy you'd picture in a nice white pair of slacks, loafers, and expensive sunglasses, while his hair blew in the breeze. The other had very short hair and was seriously buff. His muscles bulged through his sweater. He likely had a very physical job in Venice. They were seated in the back of a table for four people. They were persistent yet polite as they tried to speak with me. I got off the stool to hear them, and walked the few steps to their table.

"Non parlo bene Italiano," I said.

"You speak English?" asked the swarthy one.

"Sì, I'm American."

"Would you like to have a drink with us? It's my friend's birthday today. He's forty."

I looked them over as one of the waiters commented to them, showing that he knew them personally.

"Happy Birthday. Buon Compleanno," I replied. "Okay."

I stepped back and took my drink off the bar, and joined them. They were very generous, ordering several appetizers to go along with the drinks. It was a total flip from the earlier part of the evening. They were both extremely complimentary and attentive. The waitress brought out some cake for the celebration, but there was no birthday song.

So, I channeled the Marilyn within and said in a sexy voice, "Happy Birthday." And I proceeded to sing "Happy Birthday Mr. President." Some smiles emerged from the people nearby as well as from the birthday boy. The energy around now was like fire that wanted to spin off in a totally new direction, after being injected with oxygen.

When the music stopped for the evening, they invited me to join them at another spot. Being in a much better mood now, I agreed. I thought we were walking, but we stepped out of the restaurant to a beautiful, classic wooden

Venetian taxi. Of course, the swarthy one was the taxi driver!

Now I felt like Marilyn in a James Bond movie, racing around Venice with the wind blowing through my hair. We'd fly down the canals and under the bridges. It was a cold but crystal clear night. They were both perfect gentlemen. We made different stops around the city that were still open, until we got stuck in one location where it was all dark and everything appeared closed. The birthday boy and I desperately needed a restroom. He motioned for me to follow him and he took off down a dark alley, and motioned for me to go in another location. It was 3:00 am so most of the streets were empty. He assumed we'd pee in an empty calle. But, besides my whole reluctance to pee in a calle of Venice after a glamorous evening, I realized my jeans had gotten too tight as I started to yank them down. The logistics were too complicated. I was also still wearing my heels. I would likely fall, pee all over myself, and not be able to get my pants buttoned. I went back to the boat and stated that it was necessary to find a toilet. I wouldn't go in the street. So, the birthday boy took my hand and we wove in and out of the calli until we found something open. He let go of my hand for a moment, and focusing on only going to the toilet and not the uneven ground, I took off quickly across the courtyard and tumbled to the ground in all my glory. My friend dashed over and collected me. My feet were getting tired. My friend then escorted me to the toilet room door. Afterwards, the three of us snuggled up in a cozy booth table and we had another round. I was surprised at how lively this place was at that hour. Part of the wall was open to the outside, so even more people were standing outdoors. The music blasted while the fashionably dressed people meandered about, obviously still on the prowl.

It was approaching 4:00 am when we sped across the lagoon back to a canal near my house. They were kind and parked the boat as close to my apartment as possible. The taxi driver gave me his card, and then the birthday boy walked me to the door, assisting me in my high heels. I carried my flats the entire night, but never wore them. I was having such an incredible time that I didn't think about changing. It was a perfect night with them. We said our goodnights and he left. So, one bad date turned into two good ones.

16

REST AND BAD NEWS

I N THE NEXT days I was recovering from exhaustion. I ached all over. I don't even recall if I went out of the apartment much. I was eating healthily, not drinking, trying to sleep, and mostly worked on the computer. My sore throat was getting worse, but I thought that with rest I could push through it.

I Googled a few guys I'd known in the past, out of curiosity to see what they were doing. One, whom I had met briefly in Venice 28 years before, was named Murray. We had a strange friendship and had recently reconnected by email. But, funny how the same story never changed. He couldn't get it together to make an effort with me 28 years before, and it was the same now. He still held our connection in high esteem, perhaps even the pinnacle of all his romantic relationships in this life-time. But he never had the courage to realize if it was fantasy, or if it was real. Maybe, for some reason, he needed to keep that ideal memorialized in order to func-tion in the life that he had created for himself. It was not a concept I understood, which was why I stopped contact again. I had wasted too many years with people who couldn't make up their minds. I wasn't interested in wasting any more years. Murray came to mind because I had received an email stating that my professor from the Venice Abroad Program had just died. I had planned to get in touch with him in the next week. I was too late.

In reality I didn't stay in touch with this professor much over the years, but his death was a blow. My pri-mary professor had passed a few years before. But this one was the last one I really knew. It was a reality check on how much time had gone by since I was in school there, and how much older I was. And I was reminded of the important chapters of my life that had been left out.

My writing and music were fulfilling and heal-ing for me now. I tried to channel my gloominess into another song or poem. Creativity sparks positive emo-tions. Embracing the negative feelings, and becoming creative with them, transformed my mood to a positive one. Also, the resulting product was a true reflection of a basic human condition. I've learned that everyone experiences the light and the dark of life. Only by seeing one, can we understand and appreciate the other.

As far as the dark side, the British partiers were getting worse. Their meanness and cruelty towards others in their stories and jokes had escalated like an epidemic. I was empathetic towards the people who knew them, particularly a few names I heard repeatedly. Not all of them were British, but they usually spoke in the common language of English. I couldn't hear the conversations perfectly at all. Only if they spoke so loudly that I couldn't block them out, would I follow what they were saying. Depending on where they were in relation to where I was in the apartment, I could hear them better or only pieces of a conversation. But I couldn't figure out where they were outside. The "Italian way" was to stand in a calle somewhere, talking and drinking. Wherever they were, I didn't want to hear them. One recurring theme was about someone's CD and whether or not they would buy it. It was always the same. Some people liked the music, and one woman in particular thought it was terrible. Being a songwriter, this conversation made me particularly sick to my stomach. Critics were energy vampires.

I made several positive phone calls on my Magic Jack, feeling fortunate that I had never actually met those hideous people outside. I was thankful that my computer made it so easy to stay connected to the nicer people in the world.

One morning, I saw a newspaper stuck in my door. It was only the section listing apartments for rent and for sale. I had never received the paper before and it was odd that only that section was left. I examined all the other doors on the block and no one else had a newspaper stuck in their door. A terrible thought struck me—what if my landlord, who worked nearby, had overheard me speaking on the phone about needing to leave because of the noise? He was a wonderful man, so I felt guilty for this. I took the paper back into the flat and reviewed it. From then on I spoke more quietly on the phone and didn't mention how much I wanted to move.

❧❧

17

DINNER WITH TINO

MADE PLANS TO have dinner with Trish at Al Remer. An hour and a half before we were to meet, Tino, the person I had previously been introduced to by Thomas, called to say he was in town and wanted to get together. I wanted to see Tino because he had some job and apartment possibilities for me. After I told him I had plans, he asked if he could join us. I thought that was very forward, but I figured maybe it was common in Italy. Knowing how Trish was used to meeting with groups of people, I said it would be okay if Trish agreed, which she did.

He picked me up late, in his dingy, which was annoying since he was intruding on our plans. We arrived to meet Trish, but she had not reserved a table as she'd said. Trish volunteered to leave, but we found a way to put three people at a table for two. My intention was that we could all have a good time and watch the music. But Trish found a way to eat, and leave the table, leaving us with her bill. I was beginning to see a pattern with her behavior here. This time she used the host as an excuse. She'd whisper to him, the two would look over at us, and eventually he served as her means of escape.

Dinner with Tino was not what I expected. I learned very little about possible employment, and he kept talking over the band that was just a table away from us. Everyone around us was annoyed by his outbursts, so when he suggested we leave, I was happy to.

Now, the dingy ride was the best part of the evening. He took me down all the tiny canals, in different areas I wasn't familiar with, for about an hour. It was creepy seeing the rats run along under some of the bridges. It was a different and intriguing personality of Venice, cold and eerie. He asked if I wanted one last drink at his place, which was nearby, before he took me back, so I agreed.

His place was not at all what I expected. The flats he was renting were very beautiful. But the flat he lived in was a dump. It was on the ground level where the high water would flood the kitchen. It looked more like a college apartment than one where a successful businessman lived.

The conversation started off well, but deteriorated.

He asked if I had children, so I told him of my great loss and how I was still grieving. Then, without thinking, he pulled out photos of his son, who was close to the age my son would have been, and boasted about him. He showed me photo after photo, as if his son was his trophy. I tried to be pleasant, but couldn't believe how insensitive he was. I looked at all the photos for each year of the child's life, as if that could have been my son aging. He went on and on about what a perfect child he was. It was hard to take. Evidently, his previous girlfriend purposefully got pregnant then left him. He was in his son's life, but was baffled by why the woman left him. Well, I understood.... I finally couldn't take it anymore and I said, "I'm happy for you and your son. But it's difficult for me because I lost my only child not long ago. Maybe we could talk about something else."

He fired back, "But you don't even know what it's like to have a child. You never had yours. If I lost my son it would be unbearable. You can't compare your loss with one that was born and living. Your loss wasn't even real."

My eyes opened wide. I couldn't believe someone could be so cruel and ignorant. Tears started building and running down my face. I thought of the months of humiliation, going through artificial insemination. How humiliating it was for me to even make that decision, after not meeting someone who loved me and wanted to have children with me. And I put off that decision until I was 45. I recalled how I chose not to terminate the pregnancy when the doctors thought it was a tubular pregnancy, and a tube could rupture and I could die in 30 minutes. All along, I dealt with mean comments from some friends and even a few family members for my decision to have a child alone. But I fought for that decision. And I loved my son, Jacques. I was ecstatically happy when I received the news that I was pregnant. It was not a pregnancy that happened by accident. When it finally happened it was very real. I knew he would likely be my only child as well.

I barely got out, "He was very real to me. It's late, I think I need to go home."

I wanted to just run out the door, but the walk back would have been an hour or more if I got lost. So he took me by boat, driving recklessly across the lagoon. I think at this point he was annoyed he had to take me back, and was driving me back faster than the dingy should be driven. The dingy had the tendency to flip at high speeds, but this did not stop him. I kept watching the shoreline, knowing how far I could swim and how long I had before hypothermia set in. This was actually nothing compared to things I had gone through in the past, but it was infuriating. I asked him to slow down, which he would do for a moment, then speed up again when he got bored. He finally dropped me off on the side of a canal near my house, and I walked back alone.

I thought of how badly the evening had ended, and how clueless and unaware he was in general on so many things. My decision to have a child was honest compared to his girlfriend's decision to trap him. I thought of all the other monstrous comments that had been said to me in recent years. I had met so many dopes in my life. Even the "Mom's Club" had a serious disconnect with childless women. Most of these people didn't have bad intentions, but were simply clueless about what was flying out of their mouths and how it affected other people. Tino was not evil, just clueless. But it was painful reliving that loss.

It was about 1:30 am, and I was really feeling the flu come on. Driving around in the damp night air didn't help. Of course, once I was in the house my insomnia kicked in also. I was too wired from the evening and I knew 5:00 or 5:30 was quickly approaching. For some reason, I didn't hear the partiers. Maybe the rain, which had just started, kept them inside. I relaxed and quietly played the song I had written about my son a few times. It gave me strength before I finally drifted to sleep.

18

OUT OF THE DARK

I WAS AWAKENED AROUND 4:00 am by voices, after dozing for only a couple of hours. An American guy with a strange accent was pouring his heart out to this Italian girl. I gathered from part of the conversation that she lived at Giardini, the garden area. She was very quiet and shy. He seemed insecure and awkward as he tried to express himself.

"But I have feelings for you. I want to see you more," he said in a lovesick, quivering voice.

She said nothing.

"I care for you. I thought maybe we could be more…. What do you think?"

The girl was quiet and then just made a noise, acknowledging but still not sure.

"Per favore," the kid said, "I think I love you. Ti amo…. Can we work something out?"

She sounded happy from the mumbling and squeaks she emitted, but said only, "Maybe."

Throughout the conversation, you could tell he was nervous and frustrated, walking around, pacing, and knocking on metal that sounded like the pull-down doors over the shops. His voice faded in and out as he walked closer then away from my bedroom window. The loud clunking of his shoes echoed off the walls of the narrow calle. Then he stomped off and accelerated to almost a run.

BANG! He hit something metal very hard. It sounded like a gate.

"Oh no … oh no," he said, mortified.

He rattled something over and over. "I think I broke it."

"What?" she replied, as she walked over to him.

There was more jiggling on the metal.

"Can't believe … let's go," he said.

She acknowledged then the footsteps and voices faded out.

In the quiet, I dozed a little more until the loud carts rolled down the calle again. Two guys were talking. They passed by the broken thing and one rattled it again.

"You did this," a guy with an accent said to his friend.

"No," said the other guy. But it was the same voice I had heard before who had "done it."

"I know you did this. It's something you would do."

"No, I didn't do it. It was someone else. It wasn't me."

"I don't believe you." The guy sounded pissed. Then they started up again and left.

I thought that maybe they were trash collectors. But it didn't make sense that the city would hire people who weren't Italian. The voice of the friend came by again, with someone else, and another loud cart.

"See, look at this," the guy said to his friend. "I know in my gut he did it."

"Who again?"

"Murray, that American guy. He's always getting into trouble. I know it was him."

I was surprised that their English was so good. And I thought it was funny that I had just been looking at the Murray I knew on Facebook. Of course, it was not his voice. This "American Murray" had a very strange voice, with an accent I couldn't place. It almost sounded like he was either a little mentally impaired or overwhelmingly shy. But, what a strange coincidence, with an uncommon name.

Between 6:00 and 7:00, I heard British voices talking about the broken thing and that it looked like someone was trying to break in. I felt like I had to do something, though I didn't want to. I was warm and comfortable in my bed. But I felt it was my duty to let them know about the lovesick kid who'd made a mistake. So I went downstairs and looked around outside, but didn't find anything broken. There were no people around and just a few cafes open. I went into one place and asked if they had heard of a break-in. They didn't know what I was talking about. People gossip in Venice, so if something had happened the shop would have known. Crime was rare there, so they gave me a very odd look. I walked the calli near my flat, looking for something broken, for just under an hour. But I didn't find anything. I was getting very cold, so I went back into the flat. At first, when I entered, it was quiet. Then I heard the British people talking about the broken thing, and whether they should call the police. I was so frustrated. I wanted to explain the story, but couldn't find where the British people were. A few of the voices were the same ones I always heard. I would open the shutters, look out, and hear nothing. The voices seemed to mostly be by the window near my bed.

Again, I figured they were around the corner. I figured it must be a busy corner with the market, though I didn't see anyone when I was just there.

Another thing I pondered again, was that I never saw those loud carts in the mornings, though I often heard them. Since the Venetian worker carts had rubber wheels, I hypothesized about them being from suitcases that people lugged around. But it was too regular, being every morning. And it was so early. The pitch and quality of noise didn't sound like rubber or plastic. It sounded more like wood, or metal, on stone. But I had never seen wooden wheels there before. It was not something I thought much about anyway. I just wanted to get my sleep. I heard the carts outside, so I knew they were there.

I rested at home, trying to sleep and feel better. I was exhausted and felt like I was running a slight fever. I made a few phone calls just for the company. And, still feeling like I needed to report the incident, I continued looking out the window whenever I would hear the voices. But, each time I looked out, it was quiet, cold, and still. There were no people. It was absurd how it was perfectly timed: just as I would close the windows and shutters, the voices would start up again. It became a game. I would throw them open as quickly as possible to silence, and close them to voices. Over and over. I couldn't believe it. Finally, I cozied up in bed sipping tea, tired from it all. A couple walked by, talking about how beautiful the city was.

"This city is built like a fortress. The walls are thick but you can hear everything through them."

What an understatement, and how appropriately timed! This was a very strange morning I was having. I decided to call my mother and see how things were. I also wanted my father to review some grammar changes on my songs. She put me on hold for a second and I listened to voices chattering again, but this time they were closer. One person had just caught up to his friends.

"So, how is she today?" he asked.

"Shhh ... she's talking to her mum."

A sharp tinge hit and I felt sick to my stomach. Now I understood they were listening to me! When my mom returned I ended the conversation. I had lived in houses for years and I wasn't used to living in an apartment. I realized that some of the voices must be upstairs, or next-door, and not outside. They were louder in certain areas of the apartment, especially near the windows, which was why I originally thought that the people were outside. My mind raced as I recalled some of the mean conversations I had heard. I realized that they must have heard me speaking on the phone and knew I wanted to move, due to being bothered by the noise and late night parties. They must have been the ones who put the listing of apartments on the door and not my landlord. That seemed more likely, as it didn't sound like something my landlord would do. But they probably also wanted me to move because I was always complaining about them. I just lay there and listened. More of them came in and out, but did not say much.

Then one walked in and said, laughing, "How's Mary Martin?"

Panicky, I tuned into the conversation.

"Thank God she's not playing that horrid music today."

Now I was crippled from my queasy stomach.

"I don't think it's so bad. I kind of like it," said another.

"I can't take that bloody wailing, over and over. Oh, he left me … I'm going to die … come back.… God, it's pathetic!"

Another one chimed in, "It's pretty bad. It just goes on and on and on."

"I like it. She has a pretty voice. It's a different kind of music."

"It's sooooo depressing.…"

"Have you even listened to the words?"

"No, I just hear this wailing and I want it to stop."

I was so hurt and embarrassed I wanted to curl

up into a ball and die. Or just spontaneously vanish to another part of Venice. Had I known that playing and editing my music was too loud, I would have turned it down. I had no idea. What could I do? I needed to confide in someone to get an objective opinion. Trish and I had become friends, so I felt she would listen. She knew my music and seemed to like it. But, not wanting to make any noise, I sent her an email.

Dear Trish,

You'll never believe the cause of much of my noise. There's a hoard of people upstairs and next door from England. And they are talking about me! Some of the time. Though the relationship thing with Mary outside the door was real. I don't know why they are all living together. But they party all the time and I guess have listened to my phone calls, so they just gossip. And I think they like to say my name to bother me. It's a joke, and they'll ask how Mary Martin is, or Marie. But they chatter all the time. And I just heard one of them making fun of one of my songs because I had to play it a lot to edit it. Though it wasn't loud. What a nightmare! I feel like I'm in hell. And I figured they were the ones who put the newspaper on my door. And you know what? I haven't even made many phone calls. I'm pretty quiet. I just feel sick to my stomach! People can be so cruel. They're behaving like junior high school people. And I can hear them scheming. I'm not crazy. I wish I could be out of this place now! What would you do?

I was already sick, so I had to stay in all day, even though I was subjected to the torture of the conversations. I just lay there, listening as they spoke with each other about other people, as well as about me. I thought back on all the conversations over the weeks and realized much could have been about me. They had spoken of music and a film project, but I couldn't figure out what they were referring to, exactly. Many of them were bullies, so I did not pay any attention for those weeks. But now I was listening. Sometimes, I would hear foreign conversation that I couldn't interpret. Sometimes, I would hear Italian and understand some. But the majority of people speaking upstairs used the common language of English, which was becoming more common in Venice. And many of them were British.

There weren't enough adjectives to describe the embarrassment I felt. I was so excited about starting my life over in Venice, but these people were maliciously toying with me. After lying there for hours, evaluating my alternatives for dealing with this disaster, I decided to stage a few fake phone calls so maybe they would understand me more and give me a break. They enjoyed listening to my phone calls, so I decided I'd give them something to listen to. Of course, I was pretty choked up from the ordeal and questioned if I could pull it off. But it was something I needed to do. I told myself, "You're an actress, you're Marie Micheaux, and you can do this!" Then I grabbed my cell-phone, punched in numbers, and listened even though the phone was off. I was in character.

"Hey Trish, this is Marie. Did you get my email?" I'd pause as if listening to her response. "Yeah, I'm staying in today. I'm tired and I think I'm coming down with the flu.… I'm doing pretty well. I'm glad I moved here, though it's hard starting over. Yeah, I know.… My last 3 years were tough. This is really the first time I've been in the space where I can grieve my son's death.… It's hard.… I know.… I am trying to take care of myself.… But losing your money, your house, and your child is a lot to process.… But I am being good to myself.… Thank you for saying that.… I appreciate it. I'm trying to get out and have some fun for a change.… I know I deserve it after 3 years of agony.… Life was so intense for so long.… I appreciate that…. And I thank you for the invitations you've given me. So, you're well? Good…. You're going out later? Good…. Have fun. Well, I guess I should go. But let's get together again soon. Ok…. Sure…. Bye…." And I hung up. I had been pacing, so I climbed back into bed to listen to see if they were listening.

I heard several people collaborating.

"Oh wow, did you hear that? I feel terrible. We're awful!"

"Yeah … but we didn't know when we started this."

"I feel just awful. We've been really cruel…."

"Things happen to everyone. Her music is still bad."

"Come on, she lost her son. You don't have children. That would be awful."

"Yeah, I guess. But look at her life. We've seen her."

"I feel really badly. You should too. You don't know what all you'd do if that had happened to you."

I listened, surprised with how cruel some of them still were. And I couldn't understand "what I had done" that they were referring to. It was tremendously creepy thinking of all the things they had been listening to while I was living there. Though it was really only conversations on the phone. The only person I'd had in my house was Thomas, in the beginning, who'd turned on the heat. I continued listening.

"But who is this person? Something is wrong with her. One time she'll say she's Mary Martin and another time she'll say Marie something. Who is she? Doesn't she know who she is? Or is she just too far gone?"

"I think it's a good story still."

"Come on, leave her alone. She lost her child. You're awful. Don't you have a heart?"

"I guess it is pretty bad."

The talking slowed for a little while and I mulled over another phone conversation. Maybe this next one would stop them. So, I went through the same antics as before, but pretending to call a realtor about a listing. I said I was "Mary Martin." I made it sound like the realtor was confused who I was, so I explained that my email said "Marie Micheaux" because I was an actress. I continued the charade to set up an appointment then hung up. And I listened.

"Oh, she's an actress.…"

"She heard us."

"But how can she?"

"She heard us, it's too obvious."

"It's impossible. She can't hear us. It's just coincidental."

"Nope, she heard us."

"I feel awful."

"Somehow she knows.…"

"I don't think so.…"

"I'm going to look her up. How do you spell it?"

"It's still awful what we've been doing."

"Maybe none of what she said is true. If she could hear us she could have made it up.… Keep looking for her."

Some of the voices would fade in and out as if they were moving around. And not all of it was clear. But, now, I was really listening. I was putting my acute hearing to work. They were awful. And some of them acknowledged this. But they'd disgusted me even before I knew they were talking about me. A few of them were slightly kind, but in general, most of them were mean-spirited. I felt a little more empowered thinking that maybe some of them were feeling some remorse after my phone calls. Maybe this would continue.

"I found her … M, I, C, H, E, A, U, X. Wow, she is an actress … she's an architect … a writer … wow, look at this list!"

Now I was feeling much better, hearing that they were impressed.

"Where? I want to see."

"Here."

"Oh, my God … she's famous! She's famous! Look at that list."

I almost laughed out loud. Surely, now, they would be nicer.

"Look at all the things she's done. I don't think I can even accomplish that much by the end of my life. And she's not very old."

"Well, I guess there's a price to pay for working and experiencing that much."

This was an empathic perspective I was happy to hear.

Then the mean one added, "This is even better for the film!"

What were they talking about?

Someone argued, "Come on, maybe you should leave her alone."

"Look at this, she's done everything.…"

The nice sounding woman repeated, "I feel just awful.…"

"And you did everything to keep her from sleeping, screaming her name.…"

"That was good," blurted an obnoxious sounding bloke.

"You bugger!"

They laughed.

"There's a famous person living here and we didn't know."

"But, why would she live there, in that place?"

"Maybe she wanted to hide out."

"I don't know. If her writing is like her music she's probably bad."

"Come on. Have you even listened to the words? Get that recording back and play it for her."

"OK."

What recording? Did they tape my music? I stayed tuned in.

"Here, I got it."

"Now listen … really listen to the words, and the voice."

I couldn't hear anything. I figured they had headphones on or something.

"Okay … sad … yes, it's sad."

"And her voice is good."

"Yeah, I guess I never listened so close. It was hard to hear. From a distance it sounded like wailing."

"She's pouring her heart out in it. She lost her child. It's sad, but it's really powerful."

"Maybe it's too sad."

"It's brilliant. That is exactly the way you'd feel if

something like that happened to you. It's raw emotion. Beautiful."

"Yeah, maybe ... I guess it's ok. Her voice is kind of nice."

"This is going to be a killer show. I've got tremendous footage," interjected the bully.

"You're still going to do this?"

There was a pause, then "Yep."

"He's awful."

"I liked the one of her being carried to the door," he laughed sinisterly. "Priceless!"

"She doesn't know what we've been doing. It's really good."

Some of their voices got muffled as the footsteps increased and other foreign voices emerged outside. There was too much activity going on now, though I still made out some of the conflicting views of me. The tension continued to build, until I finally started to cry. It was too much to wrap my head around. I didn't feel well and I was in the middle of all this meanness. I wanted them to leave me alone. These were strangers who had decided to target me for fun. Then I heard:

"Sounds like she's crying."

"See, she heard us."

Then the heartless guy with the project added, "She's

just in withdrawal. Let the Alchi cry. This is good stuff."
He burst out laughing like some kind of sadistic monster.

Another guy added, "There will be other great films to do in the future. Maybe you need to give up on this one. We didn't know all these things about her. Maybe we should leave her alone."

What a twist! They were the ones partying every night and keeping me up and they were calling me an Alchi? They had to have been fabricating something. It sounded like they had been filming me coming in and out of the apartment, and recording what I did while in the apartment. But, they didn't really see or hear much. I'd had only a few big nights out, I don't do drugs, and I had one person in the apartment for a few hours. How interesting is that? Why would they do this, and how did this happen? Did they just target whoever ended up in the apartment below them and decided to film them, and create their own story? Was it their idea, or did someone else instruct them? I knew I needed to somehow change the situation. I had to come up with a way to inspire them to choose a different path and leave me alone. As I continued reaching within myself for a solution, I heard something even more disturbing.

"She's always in those jammies."

"Well, they're warm, I think they're cute."

"I like the leopard robe."

They could see what I was wearing! My mind was racing. Maybe they knew my pajamas from when I would look out the window looking for them. How could they film me in my apartment without my knowledge? What could I do? Could I tell the police? I thought about how that would play out with my poor Italian. That scenario didn't seem to end well in my head. I decided I needed to do something to generate empathy from them. I had to stage something else. And maybe if they were "watching me" they were just seeing through the cracks in the shutters somehow. It seemed far-fetched that there would be cameras in the apartment. It was also possible that they weren't upstairs, but in the flat across the alley, which was only four feet away. They could look straight into my bedroom if that were the case.

I mulled over my plan. So far, I couldn't find them. I needed to do something to draw them in to me. I needed a reason for them to have to expose themselves to me. Then I could confront them and hopefully end this thing, whatever it was. So I got up and went to my dresser by the window, and pulled out a pill bottle of Ibuprophen, but covered it with my hands so no one could see the label. I proceeded to pretend to down the whole bottle as if they were sleeping pills. I acted desperately depressed as I climbed back into bed.

"She took that whole bottle!"

"What was it?"

"I don't know, but a whole bottle, that can't be good."

"She is depressed...."

"We may have done this ... maybe she could hear us...."

"She's so tired from us waking her. Maybe she can't think straight."

"We're going to have to go in if things get bad."

"Yeah."

"Maybe one of us needs to find a doctor near here soon, if something happens."

"The hospital is too far."

"God, what if we did this?"

"Let's wait. She could be fine. Maybe they were breath mints."

"Come on now, why would anyone take a bottle of breath mints?"

"What we've got is a really good show. If we go in there then it's over."

"But, we're not going to let her die. Are you crazy?"

I lay very still and tried to not make any noise.

"She's really quiet. Do you think she's okay?"

"I'm going in for a look. I hope she can't see me."

I wondered how was he "going in for a look?" Again, I could only question if they had cameras in the apartment. Or, could he zoom in through the crack in the window?

"Her foot moved. I think I saw her foot move. She's okay."

Now I was really panicked. How could they see me? My heart was racing, but I needed to be quiet. I had to slow my breathing. They needed to be taught a lesson and show themselves. So, I fought to keep up this scene. But it was difficult to lie still and slow my breathing, with such an invasive plot going on.

Someone reported back that they'd found a doctor nearby. I was happy that they were taking my situation seriously. My scheme was working.

"She's breathing differently. She usually breathes loudly."

"Let's tune the monitor into her breathing more, so we can tell how she's doing. We don't want to go in there unless it's absolutely necessary."

They had some high-powered listening device that could listen through the walls or ceiling to hear my heartbeat and breathing? This was too much! Then again,

I knew they have advanced technology in film. Spy technology had advanced as well. But who were these monsters? And how long could I keep this up? I decided to fake a seizure and lay still, pushing them farther to make a move. But I'd never seen a seizure, except on television. But, probably, neither had they. So, I mustered up the courage, figuring I could also get in an extra breath before I lay still again. I began flopping my limbs wildly.

"She's having a seizure!"

"What do we do?"

"Where's the doctor?"

I stopped and lay still. I breathed lightly and was completely still, playing the part. I knew how someone sounded as they were dying, after reading literature from Hospice recently, while sitting at my aunt's bedside. So, I tried that.

"It doesn't sound good! What is that sound? Is it the death rattle? We need to get someone in there!"

"No, I think she's fine. She's still breathing."

I couldn't take it anymore. I was practically holding my breath through all this. But they could obviously hear by their devices what was actually going on with me. So, finally, after they did nothing, I sat up, opened the window and shutters, and looked out as if nothing had happened. They sighed with relief and began chattering again. They congratulated each other for not acting too quickly. Their reactions were disgusting!

I thought long and hard on what my next move was. This thing they were doing needed to stop! I went to the corner where the voices were the strongest and spoke. "I know you're up there."

The chatter went silent.

"I'm sorry if my music, my phone calls, or anything else I did that was loud bothered you. I am used to living in a house with a large yard. I am living in Italy, trying to start my life over again and find some happiness. In the past three years I lost my son, my house, and almost all my money. I've been through hell. This is the first time in a long time that I've been out and had any fun. I think I deserve to have some fun after those 3 years. So maybe you could give me a break. I am sorry I disturbed you."

The voices lowered somewhat, probably thinking I wouldn't hear them. But now everyone seemed to have an opinion. Some felt terrible. Some didn't. Some wanted to go to my door and speak with me. Some wanted to leave me an apology note.

One British woman remarked, "We need to give her a gift. Why don't we leave her a box of cheese with a note at the door?"

This struck me as an odd gesture that I would never

think of. Is it common to leave someone a box of cheese? Did they even know if I liked cheese? What if I were lactose intolerant? I would have thought leaving someone some tea and scones would have been more appropriate. Then again, maybe this cheese offering was standard for Brits. They tended to love dairy products.

Although many ideas flew around, some were still fixated on "the show." A young guy added, "The footage is too good to stop now. That night in and out of the taxi … what a great fall! Priceless!"

Okay, now I knew they had intruded into my life even more than I already believed. Not only were they filming me coming into the apartment, but also they were stalking me around the city. How did they do this? How much privacy did I have? And what the hell were they planning for me?

Finally, after listening for a long time, I added, "Why don't we meet and talk about this outside? Why don't we discuss everything and work it out? I'm going downstairs. You can meet me in the calle." They went quiet again and mumbled, though I couldn't make out what they were saying. So I went downstairs and waited. After about 20 minutes, I called up to the windows. "Don't be cowards! Why don't you show yourselves and talk with me. We can work it out.… Come on down. This is stupid!"

I thought I saw the clothesline move outside what could have been their window. I never could figure out how they could see me in the apartment. Did they have some tiny camera on a line they dropped down by my window? Every possibility blew through my mind. The building was confusing. I didn't know which door could be the entrance to that upstairs apartment. My waiting on them was painful. Time passed slowly as I assessed more where my apartment was located. They could have been in almost any apartment in the vicinity of mine, even the ones across the calli. The calli echoed, so maybe where I thought they were located was not their exact location. It was creepy feeling so exposed. Wanting to end it all, I waited another whole hour. Kids in their 20's walked by and stared at me then walked on. Some started my way, turned, and went in a different direction. Of course, I knew that they could have been playing with me. I didn't know what they looked like, but they knew me. They could walk by without me even knowing, having a good laugh at the situation.

I visited my landlord, who was located nearby, and asked if he knew who they were. He didn't know the people, but showed me their door. We walked to look at their windows and he pointed out that they were dark. So I figured they had left. I tried to remember if I had ever seen lights on in that apartment, but could not remember. I looked around at the lights that were on in the adjacent buildings, again considering that the people were actually located somewhere else. Not wanting to seem like a problem, I didn't say much else to my land-lord. It was too embarrassing and too strange to tell him the whole story. I just thanked him. He offered to help any way he could, but I knew I needed to figure it all out alone. As he left, I stood there a little while longer, trying to decide on what to do. I didn't want to go back into the apartment. It was nice standing there in the fresh air, not hearing the voices. If I went back into the apartment, how was I going to sleep? Then again, they had already been watching me for weeks…. I opted to go back inside, try to get some sleep, and to try to figure out something the next day. I couldn't let those idiots run me out of the apartment that I was paying for.

When I returned, I put a sheet over the window that I thought they could see through. Then I went to another window and looked down the calle. A guy with a camera and large tripod walked past with a friend. Could he be one of the voyeurs? It was dark already, so it was almost too coincidental to see someone with a camera at that time on that particular calle. As he passed, I didn't see where he ended up, so I closed the window and shutters.

Then, slowly, the crowd started parading back in and the chatter started up again.

"I'm surprised she didn't leave and check into a hotel," one guy commented.

That got the whole group discussing me and my plans again. The majority hoped that I would leave.

People seemed to come and go in shifts similar to the other nights. I had to wonder if it was planned so that they always had people watching me. After a while, the British chatter died down. Then I heard footsteps and more conversations on the calle. Someone was showing people around.

"On this block, a group is doing an experimental documentary. You can see … (muffled)."

Evidently, people knew about this "thing" going on with me. But who were these people? Were they students? I was exhausted from thinking about it all, so I turned in for the night. Obviously, I didn't sleep well, visualizing them watching me.

❧❦

19

READY TO RUN

I WOKE UP FEELING wiped out. Not a good start to a day. It was obvious from the heat radiating from my face that I was running a slight fever. I knew it had to be only "slight" because I've never had a high fever in my life. The same headache still remained since the Botox, but it was worse. I felt like I had a combination of the flu and an overload of cortisol from the stress of being traumatized. My heart was racing. The panic attacks were coming in waves. I wanted to jump around to release some of the anxiety, but I couldn't move. I was too wrecked. I wasn't sure what I was going to do. I turned on the light and sat up in bed.

"Oh good, now we'll have some action," someone started in.

"Maybe we'll get her in the kitchen."

Where could I go in the apartment? Evidently, they could see me in the kitchen/living room as well as the bedroom. There were windows all over the flat. And they knew I was up. Obviously, putting the sheet over the window hadn't helped.

I looked at myself in the mirror and saw a flush-faced, haggard middle-aged woman looking back at me. What the hell had happened to me? I always prided myself on looking much younger than I was, but this was a new reality staring back at me. I wasn't used to seeing the flushed face either, because I was rarely sick.

I went into the hall between the living room and bedroom. This was an angle from which no one could possibly see in. I huddled on the floor against the wall. I was exhausted, broken, and overwhelmed. How could such an exciting adventure go so wrong? I was finally starting over, with people interested in my arts. And I was having fun. But I was being beaten down by people who targeted me for some project that I didn't even know the purpose of.

Some new voices joined the group, a British gentleman, probably 40's or 50's, sounding a little like the actor Clive Owen, and a woman in the same age range. They seemed to be reviewing the film and project that the younger ones had put together. They acted with authority as if they were taking the project over.

"Where is she?" a younger one asked.

"She must be in the bathroom because she's not in the living area or bedroom."

Upon hearing that, I came unglued and started to cry. I was shivering from the cold, sitting on the floor and trying to hide. I couldn't understand who would do this.

Then someone added, "No, she's in the hall, you can see her leg. She's upset."

The British man in charge sounded appalled as he seared into them, "What you people have done is cruel. This person started out as a beautiful vibrant woman. But look at her. What you have done is killing her. You are killing Mary! This is wrong and it needs to stop!"

The strong British woman chimed in, "She seems very lonely. It's very sad. With all she's got, she's alone. I don't think she is even the person they are making her out to be. This is very cruel and sad."

I heard more chatter that I couldn't make out.

Then, amidst the mumblings, one of the young ones whispered, "She'll be gone in a few days."

What did this mean? Would I be gone because I was leaving that apartment or because I'd finally have a heart attack that would take me out? Or, were they going to do something to me?

I got up and called Trish, leaving a long message begging for her to have a coffee with me, to talk. My voice shook through the message, trying to hold back the tears. I said I'd meet her anywhere, even someplace near her apartment. She was the one who had befriended me. Now I desperately needed a friend. Then I went to the computer and waited for a call back. Surely she'd call back soon. She generally didn't work until the evening.

I was concerned for my wellbeing but didn't know whom else to speak with. The story was too bizarre. I couldn't think clearly. I covered the screen on the computer with my body, hoping they couldn't read what I was writing. And I wrote out my will as follows:

Last Will and Testament March 5, 2012

*I really wanted to start my life over in Venice,
the city I love. And I thought I was making a
go of it. I was excited by my music, etc. I moved
into the flat of Stefano who was unaware of the
cruel people either above me, beside me, or in the
building across from my flat. Yes, I went out for
the first time in a long time and was a little crazy.*

But it was nice to enjoy myself some. I don't know why these people targeted me. Maybe because they heard me speaking of being an actress or they had their own film project.

As you know my hearing is phenomenal. They would continually wake me with shouting my name or talking ill of someone, whom I later found out was me. It was like Sandy Barns, again, with her meanness when I was young. They wanted me to move out and put a paper with realtors on the door. What they are doing to me is cruel....

I continued to describe my entire story up until that time. Then I went on with the details.

I guess I'm writing my Last Will and Testament NOT because I intend to take my own life. But the stress of all this has made me physically ill. My chest hurts and my stomach is very sick. My blood sugar is wacked out. I also don't know what these people intend to do to me. So, if I am dead, I did not take my life. I need to make a move, but I am so exhausted from lack of sleep that it is hard to.

I want Alice to have my jewelry, except the purple piece is for Clarke. I'm too sick to even think about the rest. I used to always have plans to celebrate my life with a party at my favorite places, so people could see what I loved and why I traveled there. But it's all so trivial now. You can have the rest of my things however, and use them however. I really tried in my life. I think it was often hard for me to cope at times with all the meanness. I would have to take a break to recover. You know there's a country song that says, "People throw rocks at things that shine" by Taylor Swift. I tried to shine. But it hurts being stabbed in the back.

I guess being an artist is a bit of a contradiction. You have to be sensitive and feel to be good. You feel the bad and the good.

I hope these people somehow pay for their meanness, particularly the ones who filmed me in Venice. My hearing is a blessing and a curse because at least I could hear these people and figured it out. I'm listening to them now. And I'm paralyzed from anxiety as they don't know I can hear them. Aren't there privacy laws? Or stalking laws? Whoever these people are....

For an instant I questioned if I were crazy, but realized about the newspaper with realtors left on my door. I checked and no one else had one. So someone left it for me. It was tangible.

This morning I heard a woman say, "She's moving around a lot this morning, so hopefully she's leaving."

If I was ever loud, I did not mean to be. I've always just tried to live my life and not hurt anybody.

So, let Dad keep or disperse everything. And try to help the family not to be petty. Life really can be beautiful if you look around. There are many incredible people. It's just unfortunate the dark side of people that shows up sometimes.

I love you all.

Pib

I signed with my nickname as I always did with letters to my family. I knew they would know the letter was definitely from me. The computer would turn black if I left it on, so I waited there, covering my writing with my body until it did. Then I went for a shower.

The hot shower was safe and reviving. I knew I needed a plan. I had to stop those fuckers! I always took care of my weird situations myself. If I could handle the Latino construction workers, surely I could handle a bunch of mean-spirited idiots doing an experimental documentary. But what was I going to do? I knew I had to get out of there, because I was too exhausted. But I wanted them to think I was coming back shortly, so I wouldn't be followed. I decided I would leave the apartment and see how I was feeling as I walked around. I wouldn't take an overnight bag, to throw them off. If I was up for the journey, I'd lose them and go to Lido Island and check into a hotel. I needed sleep and to think more clearly.

I left the apartment, intentionally looking even more sick and tired than I was. I clung to the railing in the stairwell, slowly lowering myself down as if I could barely hold myself up. I stumbled out the door looking so disoriented that no one would suspect that I would be out for very long. I headed around the corner to a local bar and grabbed a cappuccino and toast, a squashed ham and cheese sandwich. The protein balanced my blood sugar levels and the calories gave me energy that I now needed. Without a clear plan, I strolled near the San Zaccaria vaporetto stop and looked up and down the fondamenta.

A man leaning against a wall was watching me. A boat was pulling up to go to Lido so I bolted for it and was the last one on. I turned to see the man making a phone call. But I was safe and on the boat. The strange thing though, was that anyone could have been involved in this prank. I questioned everyone I looked at. Even people on the boat. With the advanced capabilities in technology with cameras and listening devices, anything was plausible. If this were 50 years ago, it would be different. But not now. And maybe the man wasn't a part of it. But he was watching me and made a phone call just after I jumped on the boat.

I arrived at Lido and felt relieved. I checked over my surroundings and felt alone. I walked to Allessandro's, a friend I had known for many years, but his place looked different. His name wasn't on the bell, so I didn't know if he had moved. Last time I had spoken with him, years before, he was in real estate. I thought that maybe he knew of an apartment I could move into immediately. But I had to find him.

I walked the main street in Lido. Not being as congested as Venice, it was calming with the tree-lined streets and openness. I window-shopped and sipped on coke for my sore throat. I passed by a nice hotel, the Luna, and checked on their prices. I took a room with the offseason rate of only 50 euro. It also had a spa if I wanted to splurge. After checking out the room to make sure it was isolated, I informed the hotel that if anyone came looking for me to tell them that I wasn't staying there. I mentioned I wasn't feeling well and needed rest.

I continued on a walk along the road beside the beach. Even though I didn't feel well, the fresh air and the feeling of being alone released some of the stress I'd had in the apartment. I could think more clearly. I telephoned my friend, Franco, (a film director in Rome), to tell him what was happening. I needed a logical perspective, so I told him the entire story.

Then I asked, "Do you think I'm crazy?"

He responded in his charismatic accent, "I've known you for 30 years and you're not crazy. You're very sane. But strange things always happen to you.... It's very strange.... But, you sound fine. It would be a good film. A psychological thriller." The inflections of his voice and word emphasis turned every phrase he spoke into a dramatic production.

"A film of them filming me.... But, is it legal to film people in their homes without their knowledge in Italy?"

"No, you can't do that in Italy. But, maybe, it's not a normal film. Maybe the film is not from here." He paused, pondering all scenarios in his head with an

"Hmmm." Then he added, "Maybe they are ghosts." He laughed light heartedly with the possibility. "It is Venice."

Then I reminded him of the physical newspaper in the door, which brought the scenario back to real people. In general, I felt so much better. We discussed how I could visit him to get away. Then I noticed a small blue car that circled by me a few times. Lido is very small. Why would they keep circling around? And, while I continued talking, a man jogging by almost crashed into me. But why would a man jog so close when absolutely no one was walking on the sidewalk, and only that one blue car had driven down the road?

I asked, "What if they followed me to the hotel?"

"They won't follow you. I would question if they followed you."

I felt relieved. And even though the car and the man were strange, I dismissed them.

On the way back I realized none of the restaurants were open for dinner for another few hours. So, I went back to the hotel to rest.

I again called Trish, leaving a message that I was at the Hotel Luna, so she could call me back. I couldn't believe she hadn't tried to contact me. What kind of friend was she? I knew she had to have received my earlier message. I lay down to rest for a while. And, finally, the phone did ring—it was Trish. She sounded very distant, cold, and almost annoyed. I told her that I thought I would leave town and go to Rome soon for a few days. She thought it was a good idea for me to leave. She was curt and distracted. And that was it. She didn't offer to meet me or anything else.

I continued to rest and watched television for about an hour until I realized there was nothing on that I could follow in Italian. I thought the hotel television would have had more English channels. So, I shut it off and went to the window. As I was looking out at the view, I heard people outside who sounded familiar. From what they said, it sounded like they were speaking to a maid at the spa. I figured the spa opened to the outside area I was looking out upon. It was the intense British guy. He told the maid he was a doctor. And there was something about a show but I didn't get it all. He sounded very official as he explained who he was. Evidently, he was well-known in television for doing interventions.

The housekeeper asked, "Is she sick?"

"Yes, she's very ill. We need to get to her to help her," he responded.

Although I couldn't make out the whole conversation, it sounded as if they couldn't and wouldn't give out information on my whereabouts. But he and his colleagues were saying whatever they could to get information from the person.

He added, "She's in a critical downward life spiral."

What? I was happy. How could I be in "A critical downward life spiral?" My life was on the upswing. I'd saved what I could out of my real estate. I had a little to start over. Things were good for me now, except for these opportunistic fuckers who were trying to exploit me.

"She's sick?" inquired the housekeeper.

"She's got several psychiatric disorders. She's an addict, she's an alcoholic, she has an eating disorder, a panic disorder, she's about to have organ failure, her heart is not functioning properly, and she has a brain aneurism that could go off at any time."

Really? Was there anything they left out from the book of diseases? And they added a few other maladies I didn't recognize. But, they knew this how? I wanted to hear that part. Who were these crazy people claiming to be doctors? It was evil of them to manipulate the housekeeping to tell them where I was. This was some sick twisted game they were playing. What did they want to do to me? I also considered that they weren't British. Maybe they were from some other country and learned to speak English in England. They could have been Albanian or from somewhere else for all I knew. And that was how they could get away with invading someone's privacy. They were working from another country that didn't have the same privacy laws. Or they were knowingly working on an illegal project.

"That's terrible," responded the housekeeper.

"If she drinks everything in the mini-bar it could kill her. We need to get into her room to remove the alcohol. So please help us."

I heard mumbling as if she wouldn't help them. I had not even looked in the mini-bar. I'd actually had only a couple of drinks in about 5 days.

He added, "This time bomb in her head could go off at any time. It's very serious. She has a brain aneurism that could rupture and she could die. Do you understand?"

There was more mumbling from the woman housekeeper. She said something about the mini-bar that was reassuring to them. So I opened the mini-bar, to see what she was talking about. There wasn't any alcohol in it. What a relief! So, maybe none of the help would cave and let him in.

The mumbling faded, so I didn't pay attention. As long as they didn't know my room then I was fine. And I only had another hour to wait for dinner.

A new conversation started up outside. The nice British woman had joined the doctor.

The doctor announced to a group, "She's in for the night, so you can go home."

Great! Now I could go to dinner in peace! A little while later, I walked out and down the street to a very small restaurant I had seen earlier. I ordered pasta to put me to sleep and sparkling water for my throat. While I was looking out the window I saw Alessandro walk by. I couldn't believe I had been to his place wanting to see him and here he was. And I had not seen him in years. It was amazing I recognized him. I took off out the door. He had always been helpful to me. I had named him "my blue angel" because he had saved me before by getting a doctor to my house when I had the stomach flu. We both shared this fixation on the color blue, hence the name. He told me he didn't live in Lido anymore. His father had died in the past month and he was there to see his mother. I offered him my condolences and asked if he could join me for a little while. I told him briefly what was going on, though we couldn't communicate very well. He couldn't understand my Italian well and he didn't speak any English. That was probably a good thing, since the story was so strange. In the end he couldn't stay long. But it was grounding to see him and have a normal conversation with someone I'd known for a long time. How coincidental it was to see him at the moment he walked by the little restaurant. He could have gone in a different direction. Or I could have been looking away at that moment. Instead, for the second time, "my blue angel" showed up when I needed some help. As I finished my dinner, I wondered if somehow something, or maybe someone, like his father, had guided him to me at that time. It confirmed why I loved Venice. The Venetians had always been kind to me. It made the situation with my so-called American friend, Trish, unimportant.

When I arrived back to the hotel, the front desk gave me a form to fill out. I had never filled out this form before in any hotel I'd ever stayed at in Italy, or any other country I had visited. One side asked for general infor-mation about myself and the other side had a lot of very small print and about 10 places to check. The English translation on the form was "I agree to the treatment" in very small letters. What treatment? Could it really be something standard with the hotel? Or was this some-thing for the show and they were planning on institu-tionalizing me? This flipped me out. I had so many ques-tions. After such a calm dinner, now my heart was racing again. What was this reality show? What did they think was wrong with me? Why did they target me? Did they just need a test subject for some experiment? Could they somehow just lock me up somewhere?

The receptionist volunteered to fill it out for me and I could just sign it. She said that's what she usually did for people. This was strange. Why would anyone sign something they didn't read?

"I'll take it back to the room where I can read it, and I'll bring it back, if that's okay," I said, trying to sound like it was no big deal.

She just nodded, seeming disappointed.

As I rounded the corner from the desk so she couldn't see me, I waited and listened. I heard her make a phone call and say, "I gave her the form, but she's taking it to her room. She probably won't sign it. Sorry."

I felt sick to my stomach. Somehow, these people had convinced her to at least work with them to give me some form to sign. How could they do this? But whom could I call? I was in a foreign country. I didn't want to panic my parents, as that could put my mother in the hospital. Somehow, I needed to handle it.

When I was back in the room I tried to read the form. There was something about giving the hotel authority to do what they deemed necessary on my behalf. So, if they deemed it necessary to lock me up for some reason, then they could do that? Or, what if I had an urgent medical condition? Did they have authority to make that decision for me? All this was very scary. Even though I was feeling really sick with flu symptoms and my panic attacks were coming back for obvious reasons, I checked "no." And I went back to the desk to turn it in.

When I returned to the room I called Franco on my IPhone, which had my US number. I told him more of what was going on and that I thought I heard them outside. I didn't elaborate on the details. He thought it was very weird that these film people were at the hotel.

But he said again, "You're not crazy. I know you. You sound fine."

I told him I would try to make it to Rome. As usual, he mentioned he was very busy, so he couldn't come to Venice. But I could stay with him if I could get to Rome. Maybe I'd just leave my things in the apartment, since I was paying until the 16th of March. Somehow I would escape the crew and go directly to Rome.

Once I hung up, someone whispered, "Where did she get that phone? Why isn't she using the other phone?" He sounded as if he was in the room above mine now.

Another replied, "She was supposed to have only that one phone. We don't know that phone."

More voices debated about the phone and how it could change things. But what were they doing? Did someone bug my Italian phone? I was just so tired and exhausted I didn't know what to do. I was in the same situation as I was in the apartment, with them above me.

Then I heard something in the background. As if someone were broadcasting a television show. The reporter blasted, "This just in. Well, this story has taken a very bad turn. Our subject, Mary, has gotten worse and only has maybe 2 days to live. She has a brain aneurism that could rupture at any time. The doctors have given her no more than 2 days. Unfortunately, on the form we slipped her, she refused treatment. If she can make it through the next two days then we can end this. But it doesn't look good for her."

What? A brain aneurism? How did they know this? I called up the desk and asked for a doctor, just saying I wasn't feeling well, with no details. But the clerk said it would be difficult to get one at that time. I had blurred vision, headaches, and flu symptoms, but I assumed it was from the flu and the Botox. I didn't know what to do. I couldn't think. It was a long way to the hospital. I'd have to walk down the boulevard, take the vaporetto, and make my way through the maze of Venice to the hospital. I didn't know of one on Lido. And, what if this whole show was some hoax and nothing was wrong with me?

I'd definitely be sicker after going out in the cold and going through all that.

I wrote out contact information, in case something happened to me, and left it by the side of the bed. I wrote out another quick will and put it in my purse, in case someone took my computer. I figured they wouldn't think I would write it twice.

I heard more chatter about the television show and what was going on. Now it sounded more official. What I thought could be a college project now seemed like something major. In general I couldn't hear these people as clearly. Maybe they were deliberately keeping their voices down because they knew I could hear some of them in the apartment. But there were more voices. Some strong ones resonated with the confidence of authority, like the British woman had. She was very clear and articulate. It was terrifying and confusing being trapped in this situation. However, the one thing that empowered me was that even though they seemed to be controlling the situation and the show, they didn't know I could hear them so well. I could use that to my advantage to hopefully flip things around on them. But I was so exhausted and sick it was hard to work out what to do.

They reiterated my multitude of health problems again, amongst the group, and continued expressing concern for me. It began to make me nervous, so I reviewed the consequences of not signing the form and weighed both sides. The fundamental truth was that as long as I was alive, I could change things. If I did have some major health problem, I could be saved by signing the form. And if it was a ploy to essentially kidnap me, lock me up, or do experiments on me, at least I'd be alive for a while and have more information about the situation. So, I decided to change the form. I went out to the front desk and asked for the form back. I asked what people usually did. She said that it didn't matter. I changed it back to "agrees to the treatment" even though I didn't understand what it meant. I had survived so many things in my life. My only choice was to believe I could survive this as well. I didn't know who to call or who to trust. I was sane enough to recognize that it was a crazy story and most people wouldn't believe it. So I was alone.

I returned to the room feeling very sick from the stress of that decision.

Then the woman broadcasted, "Well, a miracle has happened. Mary has changed her consent on the form. She will live a little longer." There were sighs of relief.

I lay on the bed in the small room trying to get comfortable, wondering what was going to happen next. I looked around at the room, thinking how odd it was.

The room, like the hotel, was unusual for the climate and location. It didn't seem like the typical Venetian ornate palace. The wood paneling and décor was more attuned to a place in the Florida Keys than in Venice. Hearing through the walls was actually easier, due to the construction, even if the people on the other side were trying to be quiet.

Mumblings emerged as if they were reviewing film. The British man and woman made angry comments about what they were viewing. I tried to block it all out. My heart was racing so fast I didn't know what I was going to do. I couldn't focus on the conversation and was only concerned for my health.

20

THE LONG NIGHT

"THIS IS RUBBISH! I asked for more verification but they keep bringing me piles of this … rubbish! There's nothing wrong with her," the British doctor exclaimed. "We've reviewed it all. I don't see anything here that would make me think she's an alcoholic, addict, or has mental or personality disorders. She's a beautiful woman and person. My God, they kept her awake for weeks, toying with her. Now look at how sick she is. She could have a heart attack or the aneurism could go off due to what they did to her."

"This is wrong …" confirmed the British woman. "Why would they pick her? Who did this?"

"A woman we've worked with in New York, before," responded an older American gentleman. "The show seemed like a good idea. I don't know how it got so off track."

"But why would she do this? Why would she pick this poor woman? This is dreadful. How are we going to fix this?" asked the woman.

More arguing continued that I couldn't understand completely, though some of what they said was reassuring. At least we were on the same page with some of it. But my racing heart consumed my thoughts.

"Why is she grabbing her heart? Can we tune in more to see what's going on with her heart? Thanks.... Ok, I hear it. It's beating very fast. She needs to calm down or we're going to have to go in before she has a massive heart attack."

"What do we do?"

"Keep monitoring her. And could you put in a call to see how long it would take to get a helicopter in here if we need to have her airlifted out?"

I tried to rest, but I heard my heart beating hard and loud. I realized that they must have been in my room when I was at dinner, because they could see me. I had to try to relax and focus on myself and not become further unglued by the situation. I didn't know if this was an anxiety attack or something more. But I was very uncomfortable. And something else was going on with me. I couldn't stop peeing. It seemed like every 15 minutes I would need to get up to pee.

"Here she goes again."

"Poor girl. The stress has affected her kidneys. If she gets too dehydrated her system will shut down. What about the helicopter?"

"They can't get in here. Too much wind and fog. We'll keep checking."

"Come on Mary, you've got to relax," continued the British doctor, though believing I couldn't hear him.

I remembered I had a roll I had put in my purse from dinner. I sometimes have what I call "night anxiety," and food calms it. Although this was the worst I had experienced, I needed to try it. So I slowly ate my roll.

"Good girl. She's a clever woman. She knows had to take care of herself," he said with growing admiration. "The carbohydrates will help her."

I opened some more water. I knew I needed water as I was peeing so much. I think by now I had been to the toilet 20 times.

"Good girl. She needs to stay hydrated."

I lay down, hoping I could sleep, but nothing helped. After about 10 minutes my heart was racing again as fast as it was earlier. And, because I'd had the water, I had to pee 3 more times. I was sick, but I felt like I had medical people watching me. Though the circumstances were strange, to say the least. And I'd already contacted the desk, who couldn't help me. Surely the doctor could do CPR if I had a heart attack. But it was getting bad with the pain and the racing. I had read that anxiety attacks were different from heart attacks and wouldn't kill you. But what was this?

"My girl is worse. I'm ending this. She's going to have a massive heart attack. Her heart is not slowing. You need to get that helicopter in here now. And notify her parents that we're putting an end to this and that she needs help. I'm not going to let this go on any longer. Oh, and we need consent to drill into her skull to relieve any pressure if blood accumulates in the brain. Her heart problem could set this off."

My parents? How did they know my parents? Were they in on it? Did they tell them I needed an intervention? Wow, this was unbelievable! Now I realized there were even fewer people I could trust.

"How long for the chopper?"

"At least an hour but they will keep us informed."

"Damn! Look what we did to this beautiful woman. Hang in there, Mary."

I lay there, focused on my breathing, and waited. I thought that if this was only anxiety, I could sleep and get past it. But sleep wasn't coming. I listened to them argue more about what to do. They were hesitant to bust in, thinking it could make the situation worse. Or it could cause the aneurism. I think they wanted to be certain and have back up, depending on what happened. They didn't want to traumatize me by showing up, since they still didn't know I could hear part of their conversations.

"She's gone to pee again. Can we tune in to see how her kidneys are functioning?"

I returned and lay flat on my back.

"Ok, great. I can hear … her stomach is a mess. She's got gas.…"

"That's what that sound is?"

"Yes…. Come on girl, just let it rip! You'll feel better."

There were chuckles. I couldn't believe what I was hearing. Somehow, they saw and heard what was going on in my body from my lying on my back on the bed. And they wanted me to fart for their reality show or personal amusement. The worst thing was, that the more I focused on the situation, the more difficult it was to hold back.

"Right, there's a big gas bubble coming. Just let it go…. Let it rip! Give us a big one!"

I could be dying and they were focused on me

farting! Of course, I couldn't do it. I lay there for over an hour praying to hear the helicopter and holding back my bodily functions. Well, except once when I got up to pee. Surely they couldn't see me in the bathroom. I returned from the bathroom feeling better, until I heard their conversation.

"Oh, that's good. She had a bowel movement. She should be feeling better."

I had no privacy! This made me more anxious. Their arguing continued. Evidently, they were unable to reach my parents. I knew I had to do something immediately to calm myself down. So I decided to meditate.

I adjusted the room so only a little light streamed in from the bathroom, and the rest of the room was dark. I propped pillows up behind my back and crossed my legs. I focused on my breathing then grounded myself with white light from the universe, which I visualized traveling down through my core and out my feet as I was trained to do. I placed the white light around my body and focused on it swirling around each part of my body, starting with my toes.

"What is she doing? She looks like a guru."

I had to hold back a laugh.

"Good girl! She's amazing. Make sure you're getting this."

"She's an actress from Hollywood. They're all into this New Age lifestyle."

"She looks so peaceful."

"I love this woman. She's healing herself … look at the monitors."

I was only hearing a little, because I was becoming more centered on my meditation. Their conversations were drifting out of my awareness. I felt it was working, as my breathing and the rhythms in my body slowed. I kept it up and zoned out for close to an hour.

Although I was more relaxed when I came out of it, I resurfaced with an intense headache much worse than the dull one I'd had for weeks. I had no medication with me, so I straightened and put pressure with both thumbs on the upper inside corners of my eye sockets. At first the pain from the pressure was acute. Once I released my thumbs, my headache was improved.

"My God, she knows all these healing techniques. She's a healer. Unbelievable!"

"What did she do?"

"She has a headache. She knows where the pressure points are to release the pressure in her head. This will help with the aneurism."

A more scientific explanation followed that I couldn't understand.

"She's a remarkable woman. I don't know why she was targeted and labeled being in a 'critical downward life spiral.' This wasn't right. She knows and practices all these Eastern healing techniques. It's remarkable ..."

My heart was still racing some, so–in my relaxed state–I reached one hand up with palm open to the sky, as if catching energy, and put the other one on my chest. I focused, trying to move positive energy into my racing heart.

"What is she doing now?"

"She's working on herself. Look, her heartbeat is in acceptable ranges now. She's going to be okay ... for now."

"This was truly spectacular to witness. I'm glad we have it on tape."

"I love this woman! The more we've studied her, the more incredible a person it's evident that she is."

"And very spiritual," remarked the British woman. "We're going to have to make this up to her. What they've done is just wrong.... It's too bad she didn't have a man in her life to help her. She's a beautiful person."

"I don't understand it. She's gorgeous."

"I think you like her. So, what do you think? Could you see yourself with her?"

"Hmmm ... maybe. Zoom into those lips. Let's see

if I could kiss those lips…. Yeah, I think I could do that," the British doctor revealed.

"Well, problem solved. I think she's going to be fine."

I was flattered, but how the hell were they watching me? He did have a sexy voice and acted sincerely concerned. But this thing was bizarre.

"We need to give her everything. She's a good person. She deserves it," said the doctor.

"Why not give her the boots she was looking at today in the shop in Lido," a new voice added.

So they did follow me. I thought for a moment … I'd picked up a pair of boots briefly, but didn't like them. They were hideous and I picked them up because I was surprised at how awful they were. I liked the pair of shoes behind the boots in the window. I was actually staring at those mostly, not the boots.

"Yes, buy her the boots. But, I'm talking bigger…. Let's buy her a house. She just lost her house. Let's buy her a new one. And, maybe a blue Porsche."

"We need to turn this show around and make her the star," said the British woman.

"And put the woman who started this meanness as the villain."

"What else?"

"We can help her with her music and her screenplay or book, whatever it is."

"This publicity will help."

The chattering continued as I stretched. It was good to hear some nice things for a change. I felt like writing something to further calm myself. Expressing my feelings was a release and changed my focus. I came up with a new song I titled, "The Other Side of the Wall." It was about my situation—hearing them talk as they watched me and not knowing what the hell they were really planning.

"Look, what is she writing?"

They repeated each line as I wrote it.

"The Other Side of the Wall ...

Two lives ...

Never touching ...

Never knowing ...

Never seeing ...

Cause we're always misperceiving ...

The other side of the wall ... "

There were mumbles as they digested the sentiment. "Heavy," one exclaimed.

I thought some more and wrote as they continued–

"Still the same thing ...

Sometimes better not to play the game ...

See the similarities ...

Savor the differences …"

I thought of Socrates' philosophies on seeing the similarities in people, instead of being fearful from what we don't understand. This was prejudice I was experiencing first hand from ego and ignorance. I continued thinking of many variations and I wrote—

"Is it something to really believe in …
Manage your fear …"

I was on a roll with jotting down my ideas, which helped me process my situation.

"Is life less real inside than outside your head …"

I had used that line before, but now it seemed even more appropriate. The flow of my creativity strengthened me and changed my energy. I was feeling better.

"She's so talented."

I continued with—

"How do I reconcile the voices …
Does it matter …
Or do they really matter …"

"Brilliant! She's brilliant. She's taken this whole horrid experience of what we did to her and made something good out of it. She's written this poem with no anger. She is like some guru! 'We Are Watching You' was a very cruel concept. Somehow we need to make it more positive. Look at the example she sets. She glows when she writes. She's literally glowing!"

Another person entered the room.

"How's it going?"

"She's writing."

"She's very talented. I know her music."

It sounded like my friend, André, who was an actor. We had spoken a few weeks before on the phone and I wanted him to visit. He was trying to set up a new project that he was secretive about and wouldn't explain. But he was very interested in visiting. We'd always had an attraction for each other, besides having the special connection with the astral projection. But he never got past looking for the "next big gig." And he liked women to financially support him, or better his career. Our situation fizzled for those reasons, though we remained friends with an undeniable attraction for one another. But had he set this up? Had he found a way to exploit me for his career? Or was I hearing someone who sounded like André?

"Look at this tape we got of her doing 'the guru.' Look at the light around her on the film."

"She's so beautiful and peaceful."

More people were entering, looking at the film, and making positive comments.

"How old would you say this woman is?" asked the British doctor.

"About 34 probably...."

"Can you believe she's 48 years old? She's gorgeous!"

I was surprised they got my age wrong, and started wondering how they missed it. I figured they read it on a website and didn't know my age had changed a few months before. There were times through all this that I questioned if I was actually losing my mind, because the situation was so bizarre. But there were things that I could physically touch—like the newspaper. And many comments couldn't have stemmed from my consciousness—my wrong age, the boots and the blue Porsche that were not what I would have chosen. There were too many things that kept popping up that logically pointed to the situation being real. They also made comments that were so stilted and hilarious that I literally laughed out loud. I always thought I had a sense of humor, but they came up with things I never could have. There were also colloquialisms from regions that I was unfamiliar with. How would I know these things? I could only infer that what I heard was indeed external and not internal.

I peed again then attempted to go to sleep. I was in a turtleneck, which was very uncomfortable to sleep in and now became the center of my focus. It was tight and tweaked my head up against the pillow, so I tried to stretch out the neck.

"She's not in her comfy jammies. Maybe that's why she can't sleep."

The chatter faded out again, until I heard more commotion, as if a new person had entered the group.

"Hi, how's it going?"

I couldn't believe it. It was the voice of Trish. No doubt about it. Fuck! So now I really tuned in.

"You brought us this project and it's a mess."

"What do you mean?"

"There's nothing wrong with this woman except that we've made her sick. What you've done is evil."

"But I spent time with her. She's out of control."

"She's a typical person on holiday. Plus, she's had a very difficult time these past few years. You should have cut her some slack. It was wrong to target her. We saw the tapes. She went out a few nights late, but didn't bring anyone home. She doesn't do any drugs. She's actually very spiritual.... She's a good person. Rewind that part of Mary doing the guru."

"She just has you fooled."

"See, look at her. Look at her aura. She's like some guru and you tried to humiliate her by making her look like a psychotic floozy with all these addictions. She's into spirituality and Eastern practices. And NOTHING is wrong with her."

"But I saw her at Bacarojazz in the day."

An ally of Trish adds, "Yeah, I saw her drinking Grappa … all day."

"All day? That wasn't in the footage at all. You saw her for one instant. She came here and didn't have any alcohol. She walked around, window shopped, and she didn't even buy anything except soda. You can't even pin her for being a shopaholic."

It was strange he said I had Grappa. I don't like it, so I never drank it.

"She was having the bartender play her music at Bacarojazz. And he's a good-looking young guy. She wasn't just going to go there and be a mooch, like some people … so she ordered something. Look around. Everyone in Venice has a drink in the day and in the mornings. It's a cultural thing. So, you want to institutionalize a whole city? How about all of Europe? France, Spain, and Great Britain. You Americans are too uptight. This show you've started is rubbish. We need to turn it around and make her the hero. You're the villain. You're the one who needs help."

"Look at her life. I heard her stories."

"Nothing is wrong with her life except for meeting

you. We think she's being pretty positive. She's generally happy and coming up with artistic ideas."

"Well, I spent time with her in person. She's different from the film."

"What is wrong with you? You almost killed this woman!"

The doctor chimed in, "We were right here and she almost had a massive heart attack due to the extra stress you put on her. You almost killed her! You did this!"

"But does she deserve to be famous?"

"You don't get it. You literally almost killed this woman! You befriended her and she trusted in you. She called you up begging you to talk over a cup of coffee, not a drink, because of people talking about her in her house. She was very upset. And it was a situation you set up! You didn't even call her back until the end of the day. All along she told you how people were keeping her up at night and she was getting sick. And you continued it. You are a very cruel and sick person. I wouldn't want you as a friend. She starts out as a nice, vivacious young woman, and you almost killed her. And what about that little adopted girl she helped who you introduced her to? She didn't have to do that. She didn't even know her. But she's a good person. She is like a guru. You tried to kill a guru!"

"That's not right—"

"You're jealous! She's younger than you and has a lot going for her. You've known her for maybe 2 weeks and seen her 5 times and you want to kill her. You are an evil person. You disgust me! You literally make me sick! I will never work with you again. And I'm going to contact all my colleagues about this. But, now, we have to clean up your mess," continued the British woman.

"We need to help her with this aneurism. What you did could trigger that as well," said the doctor.

"We're going to do whatever it takes to help her with her music, book, acting, or whatever. We owe it to her. Her music is really good. We've had some people listen to it."

"I just don't think she deserves the help like maybe someone else does."

Then Trish moved across the room to reach out to someone else.

"What do you think? I'm a professional. I've done some good work with you in the past. I think this show is a hit—AS-IS. There is some good footage."

A few other voices chimed in, in agreement.

The New Yorker replied, "Your work in the past was good. But this project is unlike anything we would want to be a part of. Going after people and hurting them.

This is not good for the network. You're going to have to take the fall for this show. We're making you the villain, as Margaret mentioned, to try to rectify the situation. You won't get any work from us again. Now, we have to focus on turning this around. You did this. You're the bad guy. Accept it. We may be releasing the story tomorrow ... and maybe we won't get sued."

"But, she's lied. Did you read that website? She's not even on IMDB."

"IMDB may not be updated and does not always have everything someone has done. She also could have starred in non-union films or been in the background. It doesn't mean she didn't do the work. But I'll check into it."

"Look at this poem that was published—'*Just Chicken.*' How stupid!"

She recited in a voice beaming with sarcasm,

"I love fried chicken ...
You love barbecued chicken ...
We're all just chicken ... Dumb."

"It's a Haiku. Pretty much fits the genre. Clever ... about racism."

The British woman joined in, "My God, what is wrong with you? Are you so desperate for fame that you're willing to literally kill a person you barely know, who recently lost her house and child? You are very, very sick, you are!"

"You want to make someone famous who's so vulgar she writes songs about thongs?"

"You're so jealous. 'Back in the Thong Again' is hilarious. I'm going to print it in my paper," responded the doctor.

"Look, she even said she wrote this novel, but I couldn't find it anywhere. She's exaggerated about everything!"

"Stop! My God, you are a pitiful little woman. Maybe she did write a manuscript and never got it published. It's still a book."

There was a pause. "We should publish it! Let's see exaggerating …" continued the British woman as if she were reading something. "It says, 'It's a very important film for this time,'" she quoted. "That's not saying much. It's pretty generic."

"But—"

"Why is the money so important with this program? To just destroy a woman's life, who has done nothing to you? She comes here to start a new life. She's lost her house, she's lost her child, and you just go after her to destroy her. You need to get away from me. I can't stand even to be near you. This conversation is over!" remarked the British woman.

The British woman's voice faded as she moved to another part of the room.

She redirected her comments, "We're going to have to end this show as delicately as possible, so as not to trigger something that could kill her. She only thinks her neighbors have been listening in the flat. She doesn't know that the show has followed her everywhere for weeks. This will be traumatic for her. Actually, her ability to hear them so clearly shows how spiritual she is. She has highly developed senses. She can't hear us now, can she?"

"No, she doesn't act like it. We've changed frequencies and our volume is down."

This was more information that I did not want to hear. I'd had no privacy since I arrived at that apartment. They'd filmed me and followed me everywhere in Venice. My heart started to race again and I had to pee again. When I returned, I removed my turtleneck. It was just too tight and itchy.

"She's probably playing you, and can hear everything," Trish added like a snotty nosed child.

"You think she'd want to show herself looking like that? She looks half dead and just took off her clothes."

"She thinks she's an actress."

"Get away! Ugh! Why are you still here? You're an awful, awful person!"

I was exhausted and had no energy to do anything but to accept this nightmare of a show. They had already seen me for weeks. I was too exhausted to even react to the humiliation. They had already filmed me looking like shit and doing stupid things. It was out of my control. I was essentially being held captive. I contemplated more the possibility that I had lost my mind and none of it was real. But which scenario was really better—that I had lost my mind, or that I had these mean freaks after me? And how can you spontaneously lose your mind, anyway? Doesn't there have to be an extreme trigger for that to happen? Things were going better for me than they had for years. Well, except for my experience with that apartment and them. Also, the voices weren't in my head. They were directional. I could walk around the room and hear them better in other areas. They could sound like they were outside. Sometimes, I'd put my ear to the wall and hear a little better. They sounded like real people. Now, having Trish as a part of this fiasco made everything make more sense. Her interest in befriending me was always unusual. I reflected on all the people she introduced me to who were actors. It was too coincidental that she knew so many actors. Also, it was odd that a few knew who I was.

Trish added, "I tried to be nice with her and invited her to a dinner and she canceled. Did you see that?"

"My God, she was tired. She was tired from what your people did to her. So what! She can't go out every night."

"Maybe the 'critical downward life spiral' was describing you," replied the doctor. "She told you from the beginning that the noise in the house was making her exhausted and sick. And you kept pushing and pushing and pushing. Do you completely lack empathy? You're behaving like a psychopath."

There was more debating that I couldn't hear completely. So I decided to try to sleep again. I grabbed a few pillows and curled up with them. I was almost relaxed.

The doctor whispered, "Get this on film. She's gorgeous. She looks like an angel."

"You so like her ... Sean does too. I want to play this song he wrote about her. I think we can use it with the show," added Margaret, the British woman.

It was this beautiful song about "Mary" and how this guy had fallen in love with her. He described how he couldn't help himself and that she was like an angel to him. It lulled me to a dozing state, where I had quick flash visions of things with no meaning. I saw these clouds, or cotton, rolling and folding over each other. There was no story, only images and colors folding together. Finally, I drifted off for no more than an hour or two. In a dream, I saw these fat Venetian dolls with black hair and mustaches, singing in a gondola.

They sang, "*In the gondola, in the gondola, we can have it made, in the gondola …*"

I woke up laughing. I hoped maybe the crew was gone and it was over.

"Why is she laughing? How can she be so happy?"

Nope, it was still going on. The dream was so vivid. It was as if I wasn't completely awake yet, but still in it a little. New verses came to me easily, so I wrote them down while laughing and singing,

"*In the gondola, in the gondola, we can get naked, in the gondola …*"

"*In the gondola, in the gondola, we can have babies, in the gondola …*"

The chatter started up again. Some of the voices were a different group. Maybe their shift had changed. I never knew who I was going to hear, but I recognized certain groups. It was always a mixture of positive and negative people. I hoped that the direction of their experiment with me was still in my favor, as it was when I went to sleep. But, a strong arrogant group of people had emerged, supporting Trish and wanting to complete the original version of the show.

As I got up to go to the bathroom, a different one chimed in, "Good, she's up. Let's see some action."

21

THE CHASE

I WASN'T SURE IF I was going to try the buffet breakfast or order in. Somehow, I needed to find the energy to take the train to Rome. I didn't like traveling by myself when I didn't have all my faculties. It was dangerous as a single woman. But I had to see if I could try.

I figured a shower would give me the needed privacy to formulate a plan. I believed they couldn't see me in there. As I stripped down and looked in the mirror I was mortified. My face was puffy and still flushed and I had rolls of fat that hung in places I had never noticed before. Lack of sleep tended to put my body in shock, creating these extra bulges. I felt inches shorter from not stretching, and sleeping the whole night. I theorized that this also contributed to extra bulges and puffiness. A person needs to be horizontal for a period of time to stretch back out. I was disgusting. I had become a sloth.

As the warm water poured over my exhausted body, I tried to visualize actually making it to the train station and the trip to Rome. The shower calmed my racing heart some, but I just couldn't seem to map it out. It was too far. I didn't have the energy to do it. I couldn't see it happening. I decided I'd have breakfast and coffee and see if my outlook improved. I'd see how I felt in a small crowd of people and if I was more grounded. Then I could take the move a little at a time and abort the mission if necessary. I could always just sneak to another hotel. But I knew I had to go somewhere to get away from them. I had to sleep and have a clear perspective on the situation. The only person I felt I could trust was Franco.

I found my way downstairs to the buffet. Several people were in groups. I looked around, wondering if any were crew. There was a table off to the side, away from most of the people, so I chose that one. A good-looking guy walked in, glanced at the buffet then at me a few times, and then walked out. I wondered if he was the British doctor. He looked as though he could be British, though I knew the doctor could actually be another nationality as well. I stacked my plate with pastries, meats, and fruits—everything that was available. I was fueling up to get out of there and escape these people.

As I scarfed down what was on my plate, I overheard two guys speaking behind me in English, but with a foreign accent. They had looked at me as if they were expecting me when I walked in. I turned around to look at them, to get another read if they were a part of the show, then turned away. It was possible.

"I don't know how a person can wear the same clothes for days in a row. Even to sleep," one whispered.

The other remarked, "Steve Jobs lived like that and he was a genius."

I recalled the book on Steve Jobs that was in my apartment. And I was wearing the same clothes I'd left in the day before; a turtleneck and exercise pants.

"Women in their 40's shouldn't wear those spandex pants. Their asses look terrible. They're not 21, but they can't give them up."

"There are so many nicer clothes for older women these days," remarked the other.

"Yeah, we may have to restyle her."

"It's sad these women who don't make an effort at that age."

"What did you think of the shower scene? At least she bathes. But would you want to be with her?"

I was mortified by their conversation. It was painful to overhear, but I had to tune in. These people were real and not just voices. They were right behind me.

"No, not my type … not sexy at all."

"Yeah, I don't think it's so good for the American audience, but maybe the Chinese go for that kind of thing."

I was hurt and humiliated. How could they have filmed me legally, in the shower? And what a weird thing to say that the Chinese could be interested in my flab. Was that even true? I knew nothing about Chinese culture. My heart started racing again as I stuffed food into my mouth for energy. What could I do? I couldn't confront them. They would just deny it. I had reached my "flight" mode. I was charged. I was going to escape. I was a pawn and prisoner to these cruel manipulators. I grabbed some of my meal, and then bolted hysterically. Chatter started as soon as I took the first step. It was obvious from my terrified expression that I knew something.

"We've been made," a guy announced to his table.

I turned to see who they were, gave them a horrified look, and ran out.

When I arrived in the room, I looked all over for the camera around the shower. If I had proof, I could go to the police, or another authority, who could help. But I couldn't destroy the bathroom looking for it or it would be a bad reflection on me.

After being unsuccessful with finding any evidence, I went back into the bedroom and tried to eat the croissant I had taken with me. It was all too much to register and I began to cry hysterically.

I cried out, "Why would someone do this to me? Why can't they leave me alone?" I was exhausted and frantic, but I knew I needed the energy so I just kept stuffing the pastry into my mouth. I chugged as much water as possible because I knew I couldn't get dehydrated. I was broken and out of control. I couldn't stop crying.

The chatter started up again. The people in the room above me had been notified of my situation. Some felt horrible that I had heard them at the buffet, while others still wanted to continue on with the original show. Evidently, this was more great footage. I didn't hear the doctor. But there were a few empathetic ones who mentioned that it would be over soon, whatever direction they took the show in.

They mentioned with great enthusiasm, "The Grand Finale is going to be spectacular!"

This "Grand Finale" concerned me. What did they have planned for me? I had to pull myself together to get to the bottom of the situation. I only had myself. I had to focus….

Although it was a horrific encounter at the buffet, I had positive confirmation that the people were very real. I'd not only heard them, but had seen them. I had always been able to trust my hearing all my life, but this predicament made me question it. But, seeing was believing. Although I was in a whirlwind of emotion and humiliation, I now had more knowledge in general on the situation. They were flesh and blood people who were hunting me. I tuned in some more to the mumbling and different opinions on the show. I needed to hear just one jewel that would give me more concrete information. But the voices were at different sound levels again and I couldn't make them all out. There were many people gathered around talking. What I did gather was that they were debating how the show would end and how I would be portrayed. Although I had heard what the British doctor and woman said the night before, my outcome was still not decided. Then I heard some whispers in the background. They sounded like they were from a different group.

"I feel terrible. Look at her."

"Well, we did what we set out to do. She'll probably

be gone from the place in a day," a somewhat remorseful person concluded.

It sounded like there was more than one agenda to this game. I knew, though, if somehow I ran into that Trish bitch I'd make that vicious little squirrel squeal. I needed to sneak out of the hotel so they wouldn't see me. But how would I get past the front desk? If I had to stop there, the show would catch up to me. And I needed to leave the key. It was a normal key and not a key card. I didn't want to cause the hotel any problems.

The hotel had a long corridor with an exit near both ends. I always used the front exit. I decided to leave the key on the floor next to the door and sneak down the back stair. Although housekeeping had keys, I wanted the hotel to know I wasn't in the room and they could check me out on time. The reality show was monitoring me in that room, so they knew if I was in there or not anyway.

While escaping, there was a glitch in my plan. I couldn't get out the back door without setting off the alarm. So I had to head out through the front. But I was coming from a different location that I had never used before, on the ground floor, so I hoped no one would be expecting that. As I reached the lobby I turned my head, so the clerks couldn't see my face directly, pulled the collar of my coat up, shielding my face, and walked quickly out the door. A student type guy in a blue and turquoise striped shirt stood on the porch. As I hit the sidewalk, I was almost at a run, which was the typical Venetian walk so I didn't stand out. I turned back and the guy was still watching me from the porch. I continued on checking back at him a few times. That was probably my mistake. He got on the phone, but kept his gaze on me. He didn't pace and talk while involved in the conversation as one would normally. He kept straight fixated on me.

I picked things up and ran frantically through the streets of Lido, not knowing how to get away from them or what my plan was. Should I just go to the train station and leave my things in the apartment? Should I try to lose them and circle back to the apartment and grab my things? But they had cameras set up in the flat. Or should I go to the hospital and have my heart and head checked? I wished I could go to the police, but my Italian was terrible and I had no proof. I envisioned getting into a conversation with the police and not finding the right words, and getting tongue-tied. They'd think I was crazy and probably help the reality show lock me up. That would be my "Grand Finale!" Also, maybe some people in the police knew already about the filming.

I raced by a bike rack and thought of taking one. This was an emergency situation. But stealing was stealing, which was wrong and could get me arrested if someone saw me. Also, I wouldn't get very far. I was on an island. Not having a plan, I just ran around, darting between buildings, making sure I wasn't followed. After making my way almost to the sea, I cut back to the lagoon and lurked around by the vaporetti waiting for one to pull up. I didn't care where it was going. I would formulate a plan once I was on the boat. Of course, when you waited for something, it always seemed to take forever. I felt like I was a spring crushed down, waiting to be released. I was wound tight when the boat finally arrived. I emerged from the shadows and leapt on at the last minute as the gate was closing. I climbed down into the spot for one person, though it was a place where people usually stored their bags. I leaned against the wall and tried to hide as best I could, without looking too conspicuous. A man had watched me get on the boat and followed me with his eyes. He was now texting. I used to like men watching me. But now it didn't make sense. I was a sloth in a dark grey jacket and black beanie. Who cared? Only the show cared. Or, I was looking so peculiar that I stood out.

The first stop was St Elena, an island connected to the main islands of Venice. I acted like I wasn't getting off then jumped off the boat, just squeezing past the man hooking up the metal gate. I ran around the island not knowing where to go. I didn't know St Elena very well, except for the palace facades that overlooked the memorial park and the lagoon. So I just ran aimlessly between the buildings, until I found an isolated place behind a block of buildings to rest. Since I hadn't finished my breakfast, leaving part of it behind once I'd overheard the people at the table, I was concerned about my blood sugar dropping from the massive anxiety and all my running. I crouched down at a corner with my back against a wall until I noticed a man walking in my direction talking on the phone. I didn't think he'd seen me yet, since I was hidden.

"I've got her," he said as he approached the corner where I was crouched.

I darted off again, circling around, and then hid in a low area next to a canal. I was right near the bridge to the Giardini, the public gardens. I figured I could disappear into the gardens once I made it over the bridge. But the bridge was out in the open. I'd be seen. I stayed hidden in that position for a while. All was quiet. I had escaped that man and no one was around. Finally, I dashed over the bridge. I jogged along the path looking for a place to hide out in. The path was bordered by a wall to the lagoon on one side and a sloped hill with heavy brush to the empty buildings of the Biennale, an international exhibition area for the arts. Part of it was fenced, but I could find a way in or climb it, if that was my best escape. I passed a man walking his dog. He did not look like he was with them. So I exclaimed, "Buongiorno!" attempting to be normal as I continued on like I was on a morning jog.

When I arrived at Giardini, I cut through the bushes and trees past the children's play area. Some of it was barren from the winter, while some still had shrubs with leaves hiding the many mazes of the place. I was out of breath. I wasn't used to jogging and that much exercise. I so wished I had lost those last 25 lbs. All those flab bulges just seemed to bounce around, making me more exhausted. I stayed away from the open area and walked along the bush line. Finally, I climbed into some bushes and rested. I was too out of breath. The running could have made me stroke out. I just hoped I wouldn't die in the shrubs like some animal that had wandered off to die.

As I lay there on the cold earth, amidst the dead twigs and leaves, peering through the brush at the path, a moment of calm swept over me. My head was clear and my logical self was acute. At last I was alone again, at least for the moment. I canvassed through the questions in my head: Why was I running? Why were they stalking me? What direction had they taken with the show? Was the "Grand Finale" scheduled for today, and that was why they were after me? I didn't know all the answers to my questions. I was running because I didn't know if they were trying to harm me or help me. I didn't actually know what country they were from which might help me determine their motive. I had tried to confront them and failed. But I knew that somehow I had to outsmart them. My ace in the hole was still that I could hear some of their conversations when they didn't know that I could hear them. I thanked God for my gift and prayed for help. Then I realized the most logical thing at that moment was taking care of my health and myself. I needed to go to the hospital and see if there was anything seriously wrong with me. I knew the hospital at San Giovanni e Paolo because it was near Fondamenta Nove, where I once had lived. I would aim in that direction and weave through the city until I was there. I guessed that it was 30 minutes away.

A young boy, looking like a student, passed by my hideout. He was on the phone talking about looking for someone. I sat still and just watched. He met up with a young woman and their eyes scoured the park as if trying to see something. I stayed fixed until they were out of my sight.

I felt better as I breathed in the crisp air. I was chilled sitting on the cold ground, but I was relieved I'd escaped them. There was no chatter, just the peaceful quiet. I was actually relaxed. I embraced that feeling for a while, until I knew it was time to get out of there. Now was the time to find the hospital and get some answers.

I climbed out of the bushes, put my hands in my pockets, and did the Venetian walk. I rounded a corner near the bridge that takes you past the greenhouse on the lovely tree lined Via Garibaldi. A young guy was standing on the corner, not moving, as if positioned there. I walked by, trying to act like a normal Venetian.

"I found her," he whispered.

I turned around to look at the young guy. He was busted. He glanced back as he took his phone and seemed to hide it behind his back, as if hiding the conversation. We traded glances back and forth a few times.

"Shit!" I thought. "I've gotta go." And I took off running towards the shopping area, hoping to lose them between the buildings. I glanced back to see him on the phone, staring at me running. The adrenaline kept me going for a while until I began feeling the tingly sensation from hypoglycemia and dehydration. But I couldn't collapse. I had to get some juice. The first place I located only had Fanta, so I bought that and kept running.

I got really lost. I saw a tunnel that looked out to the water. I went down the tunnel to see if I recognized some landmarks so I could get my bearings. I recognized part of the Arsenale wall. As a student, our classrooms were in the Arsenale. And I lived on Fondamenta Nove. So I knew I wasn't far, though I didn't remember any of the calli.

Voices erupted from the little campo on the other side of the tunnel. They were talking about me. And I was boxed in. The hard walls and narrow calli magnified sounds for everyone. I knew I had to stay quiet. There was no way out, except in the water at the end of the tunnel, or back towards them. I hid in a recessed doorway, so if they peered through they wouldn't see me. Then I heard a voice I recognized from the night at the hotel. And, again, I thought, "Why am I running? They are the bad ones." And an idea surfaced—I should track the voices I recognized and ask them point blank what they were doing. I thought if I could ambush them and expose them, then they would have to answer. They would be on the spot. It was daylight, so hopefully I'd be safe. It was brilliant! I knew their voices. Their voices were their fingerprints to me. This idea made me stronger. So I listened and started tracking the voices I knew. Maybe now, I could end this thing then get to the hospital.

I followed them a short distance, but then there were other voices in the calli I didn't recognize. What happened to the ones I knew? Not all the voices were in English. But some of the Italian ones I could understand a little. The other languages I thought I could exclude. And of course, not everyone in the calli was with the show. I watched some people from around the corner. In English they spoke of losing me and made a phone call asking for further instructions. I crept up slowly and startled them.

"Are you from my building?" I asked.

They looked at me surprised, almost scared, and shook their heads, "no." Then they pretended to speak a different language I didn't understand.

"But I heard you speaking of me."

They shook their heads, looked back and forth at each other, and then turned their backs to me, yammering anxiously in another language. I ran off. But I turned around and saw one of them on the phone. And I realized that they understood my questions because they immediately answered, denying that they were from my building. English was the international language now. Many people in Europe knew some English. Again, I was confronted with the problem with my plan I had encountered before—I had never seen the bulk of them before, so denial was their best defense. And I could only definitely recognize the ones with the voices that I knew well. I confronted a few other people, thinking I could catch them up, but got the same result. I had lost the voices that were the usual ones. My tracking idea was a bust. Of course, confronting people who flipped into another language only made me question myself further and feel more vulnerable.

I took off and lost them again. It was quiet as I walked along. I pondered the other possibility. Had I really misjudged the whole thing and lost all my marbles? Was my elevator stuck between floors? Was I the stereo-typical crazy person who heard voices? I was happy in Venice. How could I spontaneously pop into being a nut job? Even though I was still grieving for my son, I had worked through a lot. And it had been a few years since his death, so I didn't have post-partum depression. And I wasn't depressed. Or, maybe I had a brain tumor.... I thought about all the medication I'd have to go on if I was mentally ill. I never took any medicine. I'd have to be medicated for the rest of my life. I thought of how it would probably eliminate the possibility of having a real personal life again. Then again, men seemed to be attracted to crazy women.... I reigned my thoughts in and reflected on the tangible, such as the newspaper, and the fact I had seen the people in the buffet and on the calli. They were flesh and blood. And the people on the calli, who denied knowing any English, answered my questions that were in English. These things were real. Also, I remembered hearing that if you're insane, you never question your sanity. I questioned everything. I liked answers. And I was an artist. I always looked at all possibilities.

I came upon a few churches and hoped I could rest in one out of the elements, but they were all closed. In the movies the church was always a refuge, though I didn't know if it was fact or fiction. But from seeing the intensity of the Catholics there, it was a good bet that it would be a safe haven.

I kept changing my mind about where to go, based on where I thought I was. I had become very lost. My brilliant idea to track the voices only worsened my situation. I had no idea where I was. The endorphins I generated from running, as well as having a little privacy, helped my anxiety attacks. But I was exhausted. I would ask directions then go in a different direction once I saw something I recognized, only to get lost again. Venice was a maze. Once, I asked directions, walked around a corner to rest, and then overheard people ask the same person where I was going. So, I'd have to go in another direction.

Finally, I made my way to the Basilica di San Pietro di Castello with a huge lawn in front that looked out over a small marina. It was peaceful there, with only the rustle of some leaves on the path and the whistle of the wind through the trees. I spoke to an elderly woman putting flowers at the door. She confirmed it was closed. I asked for instructions to Fondamenta Nove. I listened to her, but still got lost. I accidentally arrived at a vaporetto stop, so I hopped on the boat. The boat was going in the direction of the Basilica di San Giovanni e Paolo, next to the hospital. I was on track.

The stops had changed from when I was there, so many years ago. So I got off as close as I could to the church. Again, I was asking directions, but stayed lost. I stepped around a corner and rested in a doorway, and I heard people talking about looking for me, again. I looked out and saw them, but stayed hidden. I couldn't risk exposing myself to confront them in the open again. They would only change languages on me. They were debating what direction I had taken.

"She's been coming here for 20 years. She knows this city. She's probably deliberately asking for directions for a different place than where she's going, to throw us off. She's smart."

What a brilliant idea! I wish I had thought of it. The truth was, Venice was so intricately designed that even after so many years, 28 and not just 20, I was still finding places that were totally new to me. I don't even know if it's conceivable for any person to know every calle in the city. These comments further validated that this situation wasn't just in my head and a projection of my inner psyche. Their belief was not my intention and I knew how many years I had been going to Venice.

This chase made me realize how involved the show was. They must have had many people working with them. I had worked on many multi-million dollar film sets, where it wasn't uncommon to have a large number of assistants running around on Walkie Talkies. Also, many of them seemed young, so they could have hired film students. That was logical.

Finally, I reached the campo of the Basilica di San Giovanni e Paolo. I needed the rest, and time to put my thoughts together, before I went to the hospital. Saying a few prayers could only help in such a massive structure, where certainly the energy was uplifting and strengthening. After wandering around for hours I needed to feel this positivity. I hoped they couldn't haul me out of the church. Then I had a thought—this was also the perfect opportunity to make them look bad. Some of them thought that I was like a guru and very spiritual. If they saw me in a church this would confirm that. And if they were still filming me they would be getting that footage. And if I confronted them in the church and asked them to tell me the truth, wouldn't they be compelled to do it? I had written a brilliant ending to their horror show. There were two scenarios where I would triumph. Either they wouldn't find me. Or, they would be lured in to my confrontation. Of course, the option I didn't want to think about was that they could bust into the church with misled police and doctors, haul me off, and edit the footage to make me look horrible. It was a gamble.

As I walked up to the grand doors, I realized I was found.

"We've got her. Contact a crisis person immediately to meet us here."

I realized they thought I was still as crazed as when I left the hotel after finding out they had shower shots. But the running and thinking had made me clearer. I felt ready for them because I had a plan.

I continued inside. I had forgotten that you had to pay to enter. This was something that could slow them down. So I paid gladly and sauntered down the aisle to the front pew. I prayed and felt calm.

The church was cavernous and echoed. You could hear every footstep, whisper, and door that opened. I heard several whispers so I turned around and saw a group of people who seemed to have camera equipment, pondering what to do. They were clustered near the pay booth at the entry. I couldn't make them all out as it was a great distance away. But it seemed too coincidental. I could barely hear them negotiating with the person in the booth, but didn't know what all was said. I turned back around to focus on the altar, so hopefully I wouldn't be recognized. Then there was silence, so I glanced back and saw them all leave. I felt better. Maybe I was safe in the church after all.

Calm washed over me while taking in the glory of this church. It was one of the largest ones in Venice, and had been completed in 1430. Due to its prominence, the funeral services for most of the Doges (the presidents of Venice) were held there. 25 of the Doges were buried in the church. It was haunting, but truly magnificent. I envisioned the powerful energy in the place that was left there by the centuries of people arriving, filled with hope and love, even if only for the time they were sitting there. Surely that made a lasting energy imprint on the place. My anxiety had subsided. I realized my force was stronger than theirs. I had goodness and the truth. And I believed in a higher power.

About 20 minutes passed and I heard the opening and shutting of a side door. Then there were whispers and footsteps. I remained calm as I strategized. I was at peace sitting there. I didn't know if they were with the show or not, so I listened.

"Look!" a woman exclaimed in amazement. "Is she going to do the guru? I hope so, that would look perfect in here."

Obviously they had found me.

"Look how peaceful she looks…. She has healed herself again. Her faith healed her. We can cancel the crisis counselor."

I prayed for guidance and felt even stronger. What would make the biggest impact? What would be the best shot? I looked at the intricately detailed altar in this imposing hall and knew I had to make a stand. I've always been terrified of public speaking, but now I had to do this for my beliefs, values, and my life. I had to take control. I had no choice but to put myself on center stage for everyone in the basilica to witness, and draw out the evil ones who stalked and terrorized me.

I walked up to the altar and meandered around,

sizing up the few other people there. Were they tourists or were they with the show? I was right up in front of the altar, dead center, and I turned around and looked out over the rows and rows of pews. It was awesome being in this position.

Chatter started forming. I saw groups of people shuffling around, taking photos from every angle. It seemed like the photos were of me at the altar. Although they could have been taking photos of the church, it was odd that all the shots were only in my direction. I knew I looked terrible from the running and the lack of sleep. But this is what they had done to me.

"We've got to get the camera equipment in here. This is going to be the 'Grand Finale.'"

Then I heard a familiar, positive voice speaking with her colleagues. It was the British woman.

"Brilliant! Mary has turned the tables on us!"

The British doctor chimed in, "Amazing! She's standing underneath the Angel Gabriel for protection."

I was? I hadn't really observed the top of the altar-piece, only noting that the whole monument was heavily detailed and center stage. So, I looked up to see if there were angels over me. And there were. But I didn't actually know the angel Gabriel was for protection, or what he looked like. But, how perfect. It was working out better than I had planned.

The British woman continued, "She's drawing us in to confront her. Brilliant! What an amazing woman."

"She's gorgeous standing there," added the British doctor.

More photos went off and chatter continued that I couldn't make out. But it seemed positive and filled with praise. But why wouldn't they come out at this point? I stood there looking around and in their direction. Finally, I couldn't wait any longer. I was going to say something. This was terrifying, but I had to believe in myself. I had seen signs that they were real. I had to believe I was doing the right thing. And I had to get up the courage to speak. As Daniel did in the Lion's den, I had to face my fear and hopefully it would fall away from me. So I swallowed a few times as I felt the anxiety rising in me.

I announced, as if making a sermon, "I know you're here. You're cowards, evil people! Why won't you confront me and tell me why you've harassed me. I've never done anything to you. You're evil! Come out and show yourselves!"

All eyes turned and looked. I just stood strong and waited. But no one moved.

Again, "Show yourselves! You're cowards! Who are

you? What do you want?" The looks just continued but no one walked up to me.

More chatter erupted in the church as well as photos.

"Did you get that? What should we do?"

"We have to hold off until the right time. The crew is coming. But this is brilliant."

I was pissed. Evidently, they had set a time for the "Grand Finale," but I couldn't make out when it was. People whispered and stared. Still, I didn't know who was with the show and who were tourists. I scouted around for an even better position, up stage a little, in front of this mammoth red chair. So I moved and stood there. There was a small dome in the roof above my head that highlighted me. Now nothing was blocking me from being the focal point in the basilica. So, I waited and waited and waited. I was getting very cold and hungry standing there, but I wouldn't change positions. My legs were tired of the standing, but I wasn't going to move. Then I remembered a poem I had written, which seemed perfect for this setting. So, I gathered my words and courage as everyone in the basilica watched.

I recited,

"I feel like the lone soldier ...
Standing on the smoldering battlefield ...
Weak and exhausted ...

But I feel like if I can just get the strength …
To stand tall …
With dignity …
Holding the position …
The light of inspiration will descend …
And give me courage and direction … "

I then straightened, trying to stand taller and more still as the looks of awe crossed people's faces and whispers started up.

"Brilliant! Where is that from? Did she just come up with it?"

More whispers continued as if they were researching it.

"She's written our ending for us. Brilliant! Did you get all that? We couldn't have planned this better."

I mostly made out admiration as they continued researching and guessing at possible sources. None of the possible sources did I recognize.

Finally, I announced, "It's mine."

"She can hear us … amazing…."

Still, the thoughts crossed my mind that the "Grand Finale" could be people arriving in there with strait jackets, drugging me, and hauling me off the altar.

"You know after this airs, people are going to flock to her as if she's St Francis of Assisi. And she'll always be affiliated with this church. The church will become famous for this era."

"And her name is Mary. Her followers will probably make her a saint like Mother Theresa."

I laughed to myself. I wasn't exactly sure who St. Francis of Assisi was, but I understood the concept. The minutes passed and I stood still in position. My legs ached from standing on the cold stones. I was cold and hungry in general. I knew I had run off my breakfast and Fanta so I was beginning to worry I would faint from hypoglycemia. Then I heard more talk of the doctor wanting to speed up the show. He was worried about me again.

"Look at that right knee. She's exhausted. If we don't get moving it's going to give way and she'll collapse. Look, she's swaying back and forth…. She's a gorgeous strong woman."

"We're just around the corner."

I loved hearing him call me "gorgeous." And I loved feeling that he cared about my well-being, though my right knee wasn't the problem. I just wished they had the balls to do something and end it. I looked around to where they could be. Someone had let it slip that they were "just around the corner." I walked over to peer slightly at the chapel on the side, but saw nothing, so returned to the position. Then the chatter started up again and I saw some people walk out to greet someone. They were at a distance, though.

"Hey, what's going on?"

It was Trish's voice. I could barely make out her blonde hair and tiny frame.

"We've been waiting on you. This is your time. You need to go up there and explain the show and apologize to her. You owe it to this woman."

"I don't know. Are you sure this is the right place?"

"This is the best place. And also for the show. Look at her up there, barely able to stand. This has gone on for too long."

"Okay, but don't we need to wait for—"

"Wait for what? This is ridiculous! It's gotten way out of control!"

I announced, "I know I'm not crazy. I have seen you at the buffet. And I just saw Trish. Come out and show yourselves and explain. Stop being cowards. You have been evil to harass me for no reason. You don't even know me. My belief is strong and I know what is true. So show yourselves!" My conviction was strong and resonated throughout the place.

"What are we going to do?"

"She knows…. We need to go out there."

I added, "I'm leaving in five minutes." I was tired and couldn't last any longer. Why torture myself for them? They would be losing in the end. I had been standing there for over an hour.

The bells in the church started to chime. They were regal and arresting, loud and strong, and could surely be heard all over Castello. I looked at my watch. It was noon. I smiled and said slyly, "It's high noon." And under my breath I added, "My brother would love this."

They barely made out what I said about my brother. I heard them questioning and debating what I was referring to.

"Her brother, Matthew? She's close to him."

That was funny as I was referring to my brother, John, who was all about military maneuvers, cowboys, and standoffs. At least they didn't know everything. I waited a while longer for them to reveal themselves. It was the perfect ending to their show. But no one had the courage to approach me.

I realized complete exhaustion had set in. I needed to go before I collapsed. I could barely walk, but I walked as best I could without shuffling. I focused on getting out of there and walked proudly down the ceremonial exit off the altar, straight down the aisle, and out the door. I was alone, but I walked with purpose.

The sun was bright as I entered the campo. I knew what I had to do. I had to go to the hospital. But I was so cold and hungry I knew I needed something before I went, in case I had to wait. And I needed to pee. Actually, I was desperate to pee.

I crossed over to the snack bar across from the hospital and asked for the bathroom. While I was in there, peeing gallons it seemed, I overheard a small group enter, asking if I had come in there.

"Si, in toilette."

Then there was some discussion with the bartender that I couldn't make out and they left. So were they going to do the "Grand Finale" in the bar? That wouldn't look good. I wasn't protected by the church anymore. But at this point I was so exhausted I hardly cared. I just focused on that moment, and on getting nourishment and warmth.

I ordered a cappuccino and a sandwich in the back room. I overheard my name a few times from the people in the restaurant, though they were speaking Italian, so I couldn't understand it all. Then the barman came in, smiled at me as if he knew something, and had a conversation with other people in the bar. He said something about it being a special day today. There was a big festival starting up outside and it was related to a television show.

It was a special day called "Mary Day." That was as much as I could translate. The barman kept cutting glances at me, smiling, and then he stepped out.

I sat there dazed. Maybe they weren't going to haul me off. Maybe they were going to make me the hero of the show. Maybe they would do the "Finale" outside as I walked out. I was relaxing, finally sitting and getting warm. Then music started playing. It was my song. It was the one that the guy, Sean, had written about me and they'd played for the group that night in the hotel. They had wanted to use it for the show. I looked around and saw a CD player on the floor, near where I was sitting, playing the song. It was a beautiful song. It was about how this guy had fallen in love with Mary. So, I really listened all the way through. I felt loved and happy. But the end took me by surprise. He sang either, "We'll miss you" or "I'll miss you." This was ominous! What did it mean? Where was I going? It could have meant I was leaving Venice forever. Or it could have meant that I was going to die. It sounded very permanent. This scared me. Did I really have the brain aneurysm? I was shocked by the ending and almost frozen thinking it over. It had started out so well. As I thought it over, I heard a few more old but familiar songs. One was "Jaded" by Aerosmith. Now, this was all too coincidental. They were playing songs that were all on my computer. And the songs were related in a twisted way to this fiasco I was enduring. In the past, when I had a burning question on my mind, I would go to sleep with it. When I woke, a song would be playing in my mind with the answer in the lyrics. The lyrics were exactly tailored for my situation. These people were doing almost the same thing. They were reaching me through my music, but toying with me, not giving me positive resolve but more terrifying questions. Did I really have no privacy? Had they taken my computer? They knew everything about me as well as having nude footage.

Finally, I was ready to cross to the hospital. I could at the very least find out about the aneurism and heart problems.

There were several people gathering for something in the campo. Maybc there was going to be some festival. It seemed like people watched me cross to the hospital, but no one said anything. So, I entered the hospital alone.

22

AT THE HOSPITAL

I MADE MY WAY to the emergency area. That was a feat in itself. With my poor Italian, I had to navigate the building which was a labyrinth, like the rest of Venice. I registered and told the man my problems, but I left out the voices. I wasn't sure if they were real or not. I was doubting myself again. Then I sat down and waited. I watched a few people looking at some story on their phone. Someone else referred to a story in the newspaper. The stories were my story with the reality show. So I listened and tried to translate it from Italian, though some people spoke in English. And these people were sitting in front of me and not on the other side of the wall. Evidently the show had been running since they started filming weeks ago.

An English speaker explained to her friend, "There's

this woman who pretended to be the friend to this American lady, Mary. She wanted to make her the focus of the show, revealing her addictions, illnesses, and bad behavior, and stage an intervention. It would ultimately make her look terrible and humiliate her. The show tortured her for weeks by keeping her awake by calling out her name in the night to wake her up. They literally almost drove her crazy. And she nearly had a heart attack. They filmed all this so she looked the worst that she could look."

"They did this for television? Mama mia...."

"Then they found out that she really had no problems."

"No...."

"Her so-called friend was just jealous of her and wanted her to look bad and get the money from the show. Mary was in Venice to start her life over after losing her house and child."

"No.... Unbelievable! Terrible! What a terrible person...." Her look confirmed my feelings. "A monster!"

"Yes, she was terrible. But through the course of the filming they found out that Mary was very talented in music and writing. They decided to help her and make her the star of the show."

"Good."

"Also, she is a very good and spiritual person. And a healer. But they still needed the ending of the show so they chased her through Venice."

"Terrible! Film people are terrible! That poor woman."

"Terrible." The woman continued to shake her head in disgust.

"How did she know to run from them?"

"She's smart. She sensed it probably."

"Remarkable…."

"She overheard some of them as well. You can see some shots, from the air, of the chase. It was very big. There are many people involved in the show." She showed her friend her phone.

"Incredible! So, what will they do now?"

"While they were filming, they realized she has a brain aneurysm."

"And they were chasing her around Venice? Mama mia…."

"They were going to help her and have her airlifted out to go back to the United States and have brain surgery."

"How did they know about the aneurism?'

"I don't know."

"Incredible. An incredible story!" She rolled her eyes and kept shaking her head.

I kept hearing this same story being discussed as people looked at some newsfeed on their phones. A couple of times I caught a glimpse of a stream of writing at the bottom of the television in the waiting room, updating the situation. And there were flashes of the rooftops of Venice and it looked like me running between the buildings for an instant. Then it switched off. Periodically, I heard people in the room comment that they liked my music. Evidently, they had played some parts on the previous episodes.

As I sat there waiting for my name to be called, I thought of how arbitrary it was that the media could make a hero or star out of anyone. Paris Hilton and Rachel Rey came to mind. Anyone can be good at something, but without the right exposure you won't go anywhere. I felt lucky that this horrible ordeal was going to have a good outcome for me. That was if that's how it really played out and I survived the surgery…. It seemed so random and ridiculous but I was grateful. And hearing about the aneurism from so many sources, even people in front of me, made me more concerned for my health.

I also reflected on how the show had already been airing. I had no control at this point. I was dumbfounded by how much of my privacy was exposed. I didn't know how they could legally do it and have it already aired so publicly. How many scenes of me nude were there? Or of me just looking and being embarrassing? Of course, they could have edited it for one group and saved the bad parts for a different audience … like the Chinese, as they had mentioned.

Some new people entered and sat down. They didn't seem to be ill, but excited to be at the hospital. I figured they were with the show. Some of them moved to the room behind where I was sitting near the open door, so I could hear them talking behind me. A couple started chatting about things that sounded like they came from my computer. It was such an invasion of privacy! Now they had everything, even my innermost thoughts I had journaled. But I was also just too wiped out to worry about it. They had taken everything. I was totally exposed. All I could do was pray that it turned out all right. I guess in general, that's really all anyone can ever do.

Of course, the longer I sat, the more my peeing problem crept up again. I knew I had to go, but I also didn't want to miss hearing my name called. I waited until I couldn't stand it and went off to the bathroom. The bathroom and toilet looked very clean, so I just sat down. My legs were too tired from standing in the basilica. I had no energy to crouch.

"Gross, she sat down!"

"Ugh!!!" I leapt off the toilet seat, stumbled, and grabbed my pants so I wouldn't trip over them. I frantically scoured the room, noticing some vents where the voices could have been coming from. And I recognized a voice from the show.

"Crap!" I exclaimed.

Why couldn't I have some privacy? And how were they doing this anyway? Did they realize that, since I was in the hospital, I would likely go to the toilet? Or were there always cameras there for security? This was just too creepy!

They started in, "Doesn't she know how many diseases she can catch from doing that?"

"I wouldn't want to get near her after seeing that. Can you imagine dating her?"

"It's dangerous!"

Then they rattled off numerous diseases, some of which I had never heard of. And there were debates about all the diseases. One did mention that urine sterilized the toilet seat somewhat. But it was more information than I needed. I just needed to pee, so I went back and did. Afterwards, I washed my hands briefly with soap and water.

"That's all she's going to do? What a dirty woman!"

There was another vent in that room where the voices could have been coming from. I really just couldn't believe it. I knew it was all possible, but was it probable? And I had to question, was I crazy or were they ghosts?

So I said aloud in the bathroom, "Are you ghosts?"

The doctor's voice resounded, "Oh no, she's doubting herself again. And she can hear us." Then he laughed and added. "She thinks we're ghosts!"

Others started laughing.

He added in a playful non-serious tone, "Yes, we're ghosts and we are haunting you."

Then the doctor started singing,

"We are haunting you, we are haunting you …

Jennifer's haunting you, Margaret's haunting you, John's haunting you …"

Music started up, accompanying him.

"Wherever you go around the globe we will follow you, we will find you, we will haunt you …

We are haunting you …"

The music became very elaborate, with an entire orchestra of music that I couldn't write. The song went on and on. It was a joke to them. And it seemed they were making a joke to me to lighten the situation. But were they doing it to throw me off the ghost theory, to keep me believing that they were real people? Or maybe they didn't know they were ghosts.

Whatever the purpose, it made me laugh and they joined in.

I made my way back to my seat in the waiting room and waited. Then, of course, I had to pee again. This was a nightmare! So, this time, I went in and made sure I didn't sit on the seat.

There was a whisper, "Good girl! Maybe she wasn't paying attention last time."

I washed my hands for about ten minutes.

"She was just tired before, look."

"Yes, it was very odd."

I was happy for their approval, but I went back out only to return again in thirty minutes. This time I had a new system, although still hovering over the toilet. I wanted to see what they'd say.

"How odd!"

"Doctor, what does this mean? Usually people repeat this ritual automatically."

"How interesting…. Yes, usually a person repeats his elimination process in the same manner each time. This is very intriguing."

I laughed to myself that I had entertained them. They were whispering, thinking I couldn't hear them. I continued with a different method of washing my hands, which got more "ooohs and aahs." Each time I returned I did something completely different. Listening to them try to analyze why I would pee in that certain way each time was my only entertainment while I waited. They conjectured on the reasons—was it my upbringing or events from my past? I heard numerous theories and medical explanations, because I made many trips.

While I settled back into the waiting room I tried to analyze their true intentions from what I could hear. I overheard some medics in their orange jumpsuits across the room talking that they were the ones assigned to wheel me to the plane or helicopter. One of the guys was disappointed that he wasn't chosen to be my escort. They were going to act like they were taking me to a waiting room, but actually would take me to the plane.

The day passed slowly. I couldn't believe I was still waiting. It had been several hours. I continued to listen to the story, to get updates. A few people looked at me as if they recognized me, but I remained bundled up in a hat pulled down low, a scarf, and my coat, so it was hard to see my face.

I overheard that either the plane or helicopter was

delayed and that they had to wait. Evidently, the festival outside was growing and it was going to be a sendoff for me. My brother, Matthew, and my sister-in-law were supposed to meet me in London for another private plane to the US. It sounded odd that my sister-in-law would accompany him. Later, they added that my mother was going to meet me in Venice, but she was held up somewhere with the weather. Again, I was very confused that my family was in on this from the beginning. I could only guess that they were told of the original show and they wanted to help me. Though, it was unusual that my family would blindly accept something which had only just been told to them. Then again, if a well-known doctor was involved, as well as credible executives from New York, maybe they were convinced of the situation. Still, I was too tired to think of all the details. Hopefully, at some point soon I would understand it all.

As the hours passed, the story changed. There were problems of them landing and they were still waiting for my mother. They wanted the "send–off" to be bigger. So they were debating on possibly taking me by gondola or taxi to Santa Maria Formosa and having a helicopter land there. There were many variations on how they were going to get me out of Venice and to have the best camera shots of the crowd and the exit.

I noticed a guy roll cases of something through the lobby. One of the guys in an orange jump suit asked what it was.

"Prosecco." He pulled out a bottle and showed him.

Then a conversation ensued and I heard the name "Mary." Maybe they were going to stock the plane as a good-bye gift. I was exhausted and getting very hungry. I could hear some more chatter, which I assumed came from one of the vents near me. I ignored them for a while until the British doctor chimed in.

"My girl is tired. And she must be hungry. We need to somehow speed this thing up. Or just walk out and give her some food."

"But we can't be seen. How are we going to do it?"

"I don't know. Somehow, we just have someone take her some food. She's getting very sick."

"Always trying to take care of her. You need to be with her."

"I wish."

I mumbled under my breath, "I'm hungry."

"Amazing," said the British doctor. "I think she can hear me…. Mary, if you can hear me can you acknowledge me?"

Again under my breath, "Yes, I hear you." I hoped no one else could hear me speaking. The vent was only next to me, and my hearing was acute, so I also assumed it was possible that the other people couldn't hear the voices in the vent.

"Okay Mary, I'm sorry but I'm going to do my best to get some food to you."

"You shouldn't be speaking to her."

"Why not? She can hear us. We can't continue to torture her. She's hungry…. Mary, what would you like to eat?"

I answered, "Tramezzini, funghi and prosciutto, and prosciutto and carciofi."

"That's simple. Can't we get someone to get her some sandwiches?"

There was more chatter debating if they could get me sandwiches.

"She can't see us."

"I don't fucking care. We need to get Mary some food."

I was relieved that he was still looking after me. But, with all the debating, I couldn't tell if I would get food or not.

Another hour passed and there was nothing. Finally I went up to the desk to ask about the timing. Surely they had an idea when the plane or helicopter would be there.

I asked, "When am I going?"

The receptionist replied, "You mean, going to see the doctor?'

I figured he was keeping up the charade, so I just agreed. After speaking for a few minutes I was told that they had called my name hours before and I didn't hear them. I must have been in the toilet. But he would put me back on the list.

I sat back down to more conversations through the vent.

"She knows. She said, when am I going?"

"But how can she hear us?"

"My girl is special. This has been cruel for her. We need to finish this." The British doctor responded.

Then he seemed to disappear or leave. I looked around to see if anyone came out of one of the nearby rooms. But no one did. I strained more to listen, and there was another strange discussion going on.

"If she sees the doctor, we won't be able to have the party. The show will be over."

"It will take too much time."

"We've all been waiting all day with her to have the party. Everyone will be disappointed."

I tried to understand what they were saying. Maybe if I actually saw a doctor at the hospital, and didn't go off to the plane, then it would take too long? Maybe the hospital didn't know everything? That didn't seem likely. Then another thought crossed my mind. All along I had been listening to both nice and mean people. I had always read about some ghosts who were pranksters. Maybe that was what this was. And they were "haunting" me. Or, maybe, some of them were trying to warn me of the aneurism. Or, maybe I was destined to have this giant stroke that they wanted me to have so I would be with them and we could all party together. Again, even though I had seen real people talking of my situation, this was a possibility. I had never been able to speak with anybody, even though I had tried. If they knew I could hear them, maybe they deliberately set things up so that I thought those real people were talking about me, to further convince me that they were real. I looked around the waiting room more thoroughly to see if anyone was talking of me. It seemed like some people were there legitimately, but others were there for the show or to be part of the "Grand Finale."

Two people came out of a door from a room on the side and were chatting. I heard my name, so I decided to approach them.

"Do you know me? My name is Mary."

They both shook their heads nervously.

"But I heard you speaking of me."

They shook their heads and acted as though they didn't understand what I was asking. And they continued to speak in another language. It was the same as before. So, I went back to my seat and listened some more near the vent. The discussion continued. They said it wouldn't be much longer until "it was over." I didn't know what to think. Was I going to die? I realized it was time I called the US. I hadn't called earlier because I felt like everyone was in on it. But I needed confirmation. So, I pulled out my phone.

"Oh no, she's going to ruin it."

I called my parents in North Carolina. Both my mother and father were there. I only mentioned that I wasn't feeling well and was at the hospital to be checked out. But I knew something was off, because my mother wasn't on her way to Venice. So, then I called my brother, Matthew, to get more information.

"Hey Sis!"

"Matthew, where are you?"

"I'm at the office in Cherokee, why?"

Now I knew that no one had been contacted, and no one was planning to have me airlifted out of there. I was either crazy or there were ghosts. Or, there was some sophisticated reality show that was manipulating me. Or, possibly someone else was manipulating me.

"Matthew, I'm at the hospital. Something is wrong with me. I need to have some tests done on my heart. I don't feel well. And something else is weird. I think people were filming me in the apartment."

"Really?"

"But now, I don't know…. I've heard voices telling me I may have a brain aneurism. Maybe ghosts are trying to warn me…. Am I dead? I don't know what's wrong with me."

"Listen, you're not dead because I'm alive and you're talking with me in Cherokee."

"So, you're really in Cherokee?"

"Yes, I'm here working. You sound okay. Your speech is fine…. You're at the hospital. Have them look at you and call me when you're finished. I'll be waiting for your call."

I had wandered out into the courtyard for privacy, so I went back into the waiting room. There was a young woman at the front desk reporting on me that something was wrong with me, and that she had overheard me saying I was hearing ghosts. Now I was scared. I didn't want them to come and lock me up. So I just sat down calmly in my seat and waited. The voices continued through the vent, saying that if I saw the doctor, the party would be ruined. They were very disappointed.

Soon, they called me to see the doctor. I went into the examination room. I explained about my heart, so the doctor did an electro-cardiogram. I mentioned I was peeing frequently, but that generally happened when I was exhausted. I was very frightened and freaked out. They put a tube in my arm where one side drew blood and the other side could administer medication. It was huge. Then they drew my blood for blood tests, but left the tube in, waiting on the results. I said that I needed a brain scan because I'd heard voices telling me that something was wrong, like an aneurism. I didn't elaborate on the whole story of the voices. They were very professional and understanding. As I lay on the table being examined, I thought I heard the British people in the next room. There were about 5 of them talking and the British woman was with them.

I asked, "Is anyone in the next room?"

"Yes, there are some doctors in the next room. Why?"

"I just heard them."

He looked surprised.

"How many?'

"About five."

"A lot for the night. Are there women?"

"Yes…."

He continued to look at me, bewildered. But he continued to chat to keep me calm and distracted from what he was doing. But now I was faced with the question again, were these people real? There was a real doctor or nurse beside me, touching me and taking blood. And he confirmed that there were people in the next room that I could hear. And the voices from these people were some of the same ones that I recognized. Now I knew I needed to be careful with what I said. Previously, I had heard that this was "An experimental documentary." Maybe this whole situation was something completely different from my other theories. I thought of the book I had read about "Psychic Spies" and the tests that the Russians had done with astral projections. They were practicing spying with well-trained psychics. This book was a true story. Who knew what scientists were working on now? Maybe it was some kind of sick manipulation by projecting voices to people who were weakened by exhaustion.

They wheeled me around for the brain scan, then back into a small waiting room on the other side of the room that housed the five people. I was alone there. It was pretty late now, about 9:00 pm. They left me to wait for a psychiatrist to analyze me.

I listened as the group and the British doctors argued about the show.

"We're going to have to shut it down now. No one can know about this. She's not going to be able to benefit from it at all."

"It's not right. She's my girl. We've done too much to her. And she's very gifted. Where is she now?"

"She's next door."

"Great, I bet she can hear us…. Mary can you hear me?"

I just thought without speaking, "Yes."

"Yes … yes," he repeated.

But I didn't say anything. I really didn't want the shrink to come into the room while I was talking aloud with no one in the room.

I thought, "I don't care about the show or money. I just want my sanity."

I heard them repeat it back twice again, as if they were reading or listening to it from a machine. There was a delay between my thoughts and when they received the message. It wasn't instant like speech.

"She's good. She's not even speaking now. And we're registering her clearly."

I focused and thought hard, "You have a machine that can interpret my brain waves…."

"You have a machine … she's figured it out."

Then two doctors entered my examining room and introduced themselves. One was from the psychiatric department. They went over all my tests and said that everything was normal. We chatted for a while and I mentioned not having much sleep.

"And what about the voices? Do you hear them now?"

"No … maybe I'm just tired."

The one doctor was a very calm, white haired older gentleman, sort of a fatherly type. He asked, "Do they tell you to do things?"

"No … they just talk about things."

"Are they friendly voices? Or are you afraid of them?"

"I guess they're friendly."

He conferred with the other doctor in Italian and they looked me over.

"What is this?" He pointed to my lip and tried to explain that it went up strange.

"It's normal…. My lip is like Elvis'. It's always been like that."

The doctors chatted some more. I guess they were wondering if I'd had a stroke.

"What do you want to do? You can stay here and

we can monitor you. Our drugs here are very good. We could give you a light anti-psychotic and sleeping pill."

The drug thing didn't sound so good.

"Will I have my own room?"

They shook their heads. I tried to visualize how that would play out. I'd probably be in a mental ward with another person in the room. And who knows how crazy that person would be. I really needed to sleep and I would be listening to a stranger breathing all night and wondering if she would spin around like that girl from the exorcist with froth coming out her mouth….

"No, I think I'll just go home. Maybe I just need sleep."

The doctors excused themselves for a minute and went into the room where the British people were.

"Doctor, your patient next door, Ms. Martin, is part of our research. We're sorry that she bothered you. But she's fine. There's nothing wrong with her. You need to release her."

"Are you sure? She's hearing voices."

"Yes, she's just tired. The project has been going on for weeks."

Then there was mumbling I couldn't hear.

The older doctor reentered the room.

"I could prescribe you a light anti-psychotic and

222

sleeping pill if you'd like to take them with you. Would you like that? But, I have to inform the consulate, which may take a while. There are regulations. I have to make a phone call."

"Maybe just the sleeping pill. I think I'm just tired. There is too much noise by my apartment."

The older gentleman nodded and said he'd be right back.

I waited for at least 40 minutes. I got up and looked around. The halls were empty. It was spooky, like a ghost hospital from a movie. I didn't know if I would have to get the prescription somewhere else, or if I even had to check out. Finally, I couldn't take it anymore. Maybe we'd misunderstood each other.... I decided to leave. No one was even at the reception, so I just walked out the door.

▞■▜

23

LOVE IS IN THE AIR

I T WAS FRIGID, extremely windy, and sprinkling rain. I was bundled up, but the chill still penetrated every seam of my clothing. The walk revived me, as if I had jumped into a cold shower. And it was quiet from pure emptiness in the air, with no people, voices or sounds. There was just this buzz and tingling sensation I could feel within me from exhaustion and lack of food. I thought of what I had in the refrigerator as I walked. There was enough. I just needed to get back. In a way, I felt like this huge burden had been lifted off me. I wasn't dying of a heart attack or an aneurism. And I heard nothing as I walked back to the apartment.

Once I entered, I devoured everything in the refrigerator and reviewed the events of the past few days in my head. I decided to believe that the voices were either ghosts or in my head, even though I heard them out of my head. I was going to ignore them and not act on anything they said. Of course, this was denying all the physical things I had seen that validated they were human but it seemed the best approach. I had not actually had any physical contact or direct conversations with them.

I called Matthew and Franco, and discussed my test results in a very calm and coherent way. I told them that I would try to sleep and see if I was better the next day. They were very concerned, but I said that I would contact them first thing in the morning.

As I removed my coat and got comfortable, I realized I still had the tube in my arm from the blood draw. I had never had something like this in my arm and I didn't know if I would bleed out or not if I took it out. I didn't know if there was a proper way to do it, since it was a different tube than what I had seen in the US. But I couldn't leave it in there. And I sure as hell wasn't going back to the hospital. So I slowly removed it and put pressure on the insertion point, and finally the bleeding stopped.

I climbed into bed and heard people pass by the windows on the path outside talking. They were mean hateful voices. They talked of how the American woman lived there and made a scene at the Basilica di San Giovanni e Paolo. Several groups went by discussing my situation.

Some spoke in English, some in Italian, some in other languages where I only understood a few words, like my name. It was all the same topic, but stated a little differently each time. And strangely, every group commented on what a beautiful woman I was. This I found particularly strange. I didn't feel so beautiful at this point and I had seen myself in the mirror.

On one occasion a man came by and I heard him contact my landlord next door. His voice resounded below my kitchen window. "Your tenant, Mary Martin, was just in my care at the hospital. She is very sick and she escaped. I think she could be dangerous. We need her back to do electric shock treatment to help her."

There was banter back and forth that I just ignored, trying to repress the anxiety. Then another group arrived to see him.

A foreigner spoke in broken English, "We've seen the medical records of the person staying in your apartment. She's crazy. Her DNA suggests that she's likely to become a serial killer."

Really? Now this was good. It was so far out there that it had to be a prank. It was completely absurd.

"For only €300 we can get five people to go into her apartment, take her out quickly where no one will see, and drown her in the lagoon. It's very important! You don't

want people to know this person was in your apartment….
We just need your key."

They continued the conversation back and forth,
pleading to my landlord that he would be doing a great ser-
vice to get rid of someone before she started to murder people. And it was definite that this was in the future. There
were many more similar conversations that I ignored. This
again made me think that they were ghosts who wanted to
scare me so I would leave.

Then the British man and woman came back. They
sounded like they were upstairs. There were about five of
them, in a different group, who sounded intelligent and
compassionate.

I asked, "Are you angels?"

For the first time, the British guy didn't ridicule it like
the ghost hypothesis. He said, "Smart girl."

He was the only one who seemed to care about me
and wanted to protect me. "You're like Superman. But a
British Superman," I told him.

The British woman laughed and replied, "She likes
you. Now she's calling you British Superman."

I could hear British Superman give a happy, embarrassed chuckle. I continued to listen to the nice ones with
all their continued comments of how special I was, which
blocked out the people on the sidewalk calling me crazy.

This calmed me down. Rationally, I thought that even if they weren't real, and only in my head somehow, that focusing on the voices that were nice and not the mean ones was best for my health. And although I couldn't determine who exactly the nice ones were, they were always supportive and gave me strength to endure this thing I was enduring. They gave me hope.

Then they quieted down, so I couldn't hear them, and voices on the other side of the wall behind my head started up. I was sitting up in bed now.

An older British man cleared his throat and spoke with a friend, "Her father is a very important man in the United States. She used to be interesting as an actress. People in Venice liked her. But now she's nothing. A nobody. She's just a disappointment to her family. The Venetian people don't need more trash living here. She was a complete embarrassment, running around town and at the church. She's literally crazy. We need to help out Stefano and somehow get her out of his apartment and Venice for good."

Those words cut deep. I did feel badly about myself and losing so much in real estate, and having to start over. But I was trying. The real estate market hurt many, many people, not just me. And who were they to judge me? At that point, I wasn't planning on leaving Venice. If I needed help I was going to get it there. Finally, the mean old people in the flat behind me quieted down. They had made their point that I wasn't wanted there. Then the conversations from the people on the sidewalk started entering my barrier again. It was the same thing, pointing out the apartment of the crazy but beautiful woman.

I went into the kitchen for some water and, thankfully, the nice ones resurfaced. They were more easily heard at that end of the apartment now. Their conversation centered on how awful and mean the other people were in the building.

"They were purposefully cruel when she deserves the best. She's a good person, who never wants to hurt people. She has a conscience."

"He's fallen in love with her."

"Ah … that's so sweet…. Sean is quite fond of her as well. But I thought no one could get to you."

"He's got it bad, I think."

"Well … she's a very special person," said British Superman. "And she's very courageous. All along she tried to confront the others to work something out. What was done to her is incomprehensible."

"What are you going to do?"

"I don't know."

"You'd have to leave the job."

"How do I do that?"

I decided to sit for a while and continue listening. So, I sat on the sofa near the kitchen and strained to hear more.

"I love this woman. But once she gets treatment she'll forget me."

"Maybe not. You both have a very strong bond with one another. Though, it's a peculiar situation."

"But I never showed up."

"You couldn't."

"I would love to be able to just walk up to her and tell her how I feel."

"What would you say?"

"I would walk up and just say … I love you and I always have. I want to always be beside you and share every day with you. I want to be there for you and watch over you for the rest of our lives … forever."

They were the most beautiful words I had ever heard. My eyes started to tear. No one had ever said those things to me.

"But how can you leave here?"

"You could probably go and meet her for a weekend."

"That would be too difficult to only see her for a weekend. I would want more. And I wouldn't want to hurt her."

"You could leave …"

"I'd have to take someone else's body."

"But, eventually, you'd have to either leave her or die."

"I'd have to die. I could never leave her. I could never hurt her like that. She's been too hurt in this life. I want her to love me and know that I would always be there for her if I could be. But that would also hurt her in the end…. I don't know."

"He's got it bad."

"But it's better to have something perfect for some time than never to find it," said another.

"I know. I just want her to always be happy from now on."

"You've thought about this."

"He really loves her."

"Yes…. And I think for a wedding gift I'll give her a zebra."

"A zebra?"

"Anyone can give someone a horse. But a zebra … she's too special to have something ordinary."

The sentiment was overwhelming, but I would have never thought of giving someone a zebra. Where did he come up with this? And what would I do with a zebra? Would we have a back yard to keep the zebra?

"And I think we'd take a yacht down to Spain and Portugal. Or wherever she wanted to go."

Spain wouldn't have been my choice, but Portugal sounded interesting.

"That sounds fabulous. She needs a man to help her now."

"And I would support her arts. I would give her everything. She deserves it."

My eyes filled again as a few teardrops rolled down my face. I tried not to be obvious.

"Look at her. I think she could hear you."

"I'm not surprised. She's special."

"And you have a special connection."

"Mary, can you hear me?" he asked.

"Yes," I replied. "But where would we live?"

"Wherever you want. We'll have several houses scattered around the globe."

"Be sure to pick a hot young body…. And I like the sexy British voice."

He laughed, "Ok, I will … I'll remember that."

"Aw, she's fallen for him also … I guess in the end, all that really matters is a little kindness," said the British woman.

I was blushing, being part of this discourse. The last comment was a little corny, but what profound words they were.

British Superman was silent for a moment, contemplating. "She's right. She needs to be attracted to me or she won't spend the time to recognize me."

"But soul love is powerful. Do you really think she'll forget you when she has treatment? Look at the two of you. It's so beautiful … but so sad."

"I don't know. The influence of other people can be strong, particularly doctors. They will try to convince her that it was in her head."

"Where would you meet her?"

"Either Nashville or Venice, probably."

The voices faded and all I heard was mumbling I couldn't make out, so I got ready for bed. I brushed my teeth then put on my pajamas. But, as I put on my pajamas, I stared at the print. It was a zebra print. I had bought them because they were warm flannel and a little sexy. I hadn't really thought about what kind of animal print it was. I realized British Superman must have thought that I liked zebras, which was why I had the pajamas. In actuality, I was indifferent to zebras, though I loved his rationale.

I climbed into bed. The rain had picked up, so it was quiet. I focused my thoughts on the love I'd felt from British Superman and blocked out everything else. And I went to sleep.

24

WAKE UP CALL

I AWOKE TO A feeling I hadn't experienced in a while. I had slept well. The sheets seemed to be the perfect temperature, and my sore body throbbed on the soft comfortable mattress. It was quiet and still in the room as I began to stretch. The days before were so horrifying it almost felt like a dream. And it was all behind me. Could what had happened to me be over? Was the good night's sleep all I'd needed? I felt only peace and joy, thinking back on the love that British Superman sent out to me. I moved to prop myself up and open my eyes.

"You're a crazy person!" a voice exclaimed from across the room.

Shit! They were still here! Why was this happening? I felt great. I mean, I wasn't caught up on all my sleep, but I felt so much better. Chatter began to pick up from the room upstairs again. I decided to write a letter to my landlord explaining the situation. We had an honest and good friendship, though I didn't know him that well. I had decided that I would just seek treatment at the hospital. The elderly doctor seemed nice. But before I sent it out, I emailed Trish for advice. I decided to eliminate the possibility that she was part of a reality show. And to my surprise, she emailed me back quickly, asking for me to call her.

"Who is she dialing?"

"She's dialing Trish."

"She can't trust Trish, why would she do that?"

"Now she thinks she's crazy and Trish wasn't a part of it."

"That's foolish. Trish wouldn't help her before, why now?"

"She'll hurt her."

I told Trish I had been at the hospital. She advised me to go back to the United States where I had family and I could understand the language better. Of course, there are two sides to this suggestion. She was either sincerely offering an opinion of what she would do, or she just wanted me out of town. There were many reasons she could have wanted me out of town, aside from the sinister reality show plot. I scanned my brain for all the possibilities that her behavior had shown me. What was even a little more over the top, was that she offered to help with the logistics of my leaving. I had several bags, and getting to the airport would be difficult.

I thought about it. Overall, I didn't want to draw attention to myself. I would rather sneak out. I weighed my options, looking at the result I needed and the easiest way to get it. It seemed easiest to trust her, accept her help, and go back. I had to go back anyway in a few months for my visa.

I called Franco and my brother, Matthew, and informed them of my decision. Then Trish worked to change my ticket. It was a long arduous process that took many hours. I was surprised how hard Trish was working for me to get me out of town, when she couldn't make time for a cup of coffee when I was crying on the phone to her before. Either she realized the seriousness of the situation, or there was something else I wasn't aware of.

It turned out that I couldn't leave right away, but had to wait an extra day. I tried not to think about what could be in store for me my last night at the apartment. But, I hoped British Superman would keep me safe and focused.

I went out to shop for an extra suitcase, have lunch,

and get cash. I heard nothing. No one followed me. I was in a high level of stress and paranoid about it starting up again, but I walked around Venice alone.

Finally, the sun was going down and it was time to stay in the apartment for the evening. I entered and continued getting fully organized.

"She's back…."

"She'll be gone tomorrow," a voice said with excitement.

Okay, here it goes again.

"Poor Mary, she looks better today, but she's so tired," said the British woman.

I was glad to hear her voice and not just the mean ones. I also knew British Superman would be around. I yearned to hear his sexy voice and compliments. I went from room to room packing things up and putting my suitcases in the living room. Then I realized I'd misplaced my fanny pack, which held my wallet. I went from room to room looking everywhere. Back and forth about 5 times.

"What's she looking for?" asked British Superman.

I was so happy to hear his voice. He was still watching over me.

"I don't know," answered the British woman.

"Oh, she's looking for her money belt. It's under the suitcase in the living room."

I went into the living room, and my bag had turned over, covering up my fanny pack. Unbelievable! I smiled.

"Thanks."

"She heard you.... I think she loves you too."

I was embarrassed but happy. I continued to block out the mean voices that were accumulating for the night as the evening progressed. My brain felt fuzzy from everything, so I focused the best I could. And I enjoyed the comments of British Superman and feeling his company.

"You know I've always been with you. Remember that time when you slipped in the boat in Miami? I was there."

I had to think about what he was talking about. Then I remembered falling in the boat I'd sailed on regularly the year before, and hurting my back. I was lucky it wasn't much worse. But what a profound thought that I was never really alone. This sexy sounding angel, or whatever he was, was with me. Or could he have been higher than an angel? I felt more secure about my situation. I did not have the fear I experienced when I first found out I was being watched and filmed for the show. I decided to focus on this secure feeling as the evening grew later.

"You are going to be alright now. This is the last

conversation we'll be having. You will probably forget me once you return to the United States."

I thought hard, "No, I won't! But you won't come be with me?"

"I am here and won't forget about you. Just remember, I want to be with you."

He didn't answer my question.... I didn't want to stop speaking with him, but I knew I had to stop hearing the voices. I could not function on two planes simultaneously because I couldn't see the wall between them. I couldn't go through life not able to differentiate between who was human, and who wasn't.

I got ready for bed. The same mean voices and nice ones, though not the angels, continued to talk about me and argue. Some were walking outside talking and some were upstairs talking. But I was filled with so much love from the words of British Superman that I was undisturbed. I just didn't listen, and went to sleep.

25

THE FLIGHT BACK

March 8th

TRISH MET ME around 7:30 am to assist me to the airport. I believe I only heard one voice before I left. I still had the usual headache from the Botox and some achiness. But my general health was improved from the rest, though my stress level was high, knowing I had a long complicated day ahead of me.

We took the vaporetto to the airport, which took over an hour. I was frightened about going through the process at the airport, but relieved Trish was with me. Again, I figured if I just stayed focused I'd be okay. I tried to explain the story some to Trish to pass the time. She listened with a mortified look on her face, but when she pulled out her Rescue Remedy to calm her nerves, I realized I needed to be more reserved. I'm sure, in her mind, she was escorting a crazy person and couldn't wait to get away from me. During some long silences I overheard a conversation behind us.... They were back.

"That's Mary. She's crazy. She's beautiful, but she's crazy."

I told Trish people were talking about me behind us. Her eyes got wider than I'd ever seen before, and then they darted around as if instinctively looking for an escape. But she said nothing. She was terrified. I changed the topic and brought up something totally unrelated.

The airport was difficult because the Internet booking agency didn't inform me properly about the fees for changing my ticket. It was a long wait trying to sort out everything again. And Trish was pretty antsy. She obviously did not want to be there and asked if she could leave, even though I had a pile of bags and no trolley. Her cold nature had returned. She wanted to honor her offer to help me, but do only enough to ease her conscience. I did understand that she could have been afraid of me on some level. Though, if the tables were turned, I would have stayed until I saw her walk through security. But she helped me until I felt like I could focus my way through the rest of it. That was a tough call for me and I took on more than I would have liked. But I didn't want to force someone to help me who obviously didn't want to be there with me. So she left, and I was thankful for the help she did give me.

Once I finally reached my seat, I was relieved. I got adjusted in my seat and relaxed. Maybe it was over. Then I heard someone behind me.

"Excuse me. That's Mary Martin up there. She has a bomb on the plane. You need to do something."

Then there was a lot of whispering, as if someone was speaking with a flight attendant. I just ignored it, but I prayed this wouldn't continue the entire flight.

As we were taking off, I peered out the window. It was a wet, misty gray day. There was a horse and wagon with large wooden wheels in the slight fog on the mainland. I stared at it, knowing how strange it was. It was something from another era. As we took off, the image faded until it disappeared. I settled back into my seat, wondering how I was going to make it through all the plane changes and hours. I was traveling for about 24 hours. My headache was so extreme it was as if I could only see, or think, out of the top front center of my head, and I had too bricks on either side. I would just focus on each link at a time until I was at the end. That's all I could do.

Finally, I made it back, but feeling a little sick. I had peed constantly the whole way. But I didn't hear another voice on the airplane or in another airport. It was as if the last scene of my story was the period in time I witnessed with the horse and wagon. When it disappeared, as the plane took off, so did everything connected to my story.

In North Carolina, I was greeted by my brother, John. He told me he loved me and we chatted about various things as he helped me with my bags. Later, he said, "Well … you're not crazy. I could tell that from our first conversation." John also had some "gifts," so my ghost theory wasn't a strange concept for him. Anyway, the next day I was to face many various doctors. So I went to bed as soon as I got to my parents' house. I had a good night's sleep.

❧❦❧

26

DOCTORS' DIAGNOSES

ON MARCH 9TH, I spent all day with doctors, having many tests done, including brain scans (again) and more blood work to check for toxins. I spent around 10 hours getting multiple diagnoses from the urgent care and the hospital. The only thing that they found wrong with me was a slight bladder infection. And they prescribed me strong antibiotics. I have no idea what gave me one, except that it was another side effect to the Botox or because I had been having long periods. With the parade of doctors, none of them suspected any mental disorders. Schizophrenia onset is extremely rare for people over 40, with the average age of onset between 18 and 25. Also I had not heard any more voices. And I had not had any medication not to hear them. I had to wait for some final blood work related to diseases connected to insect bites, spider bites, and parasites, but the critical examinations were done.

My brother, John, stayed with me most of the day chatting, amazed by the story. He actually enjoyed hearing the details, which made me feel better. Finally, as I was leaving, I asked the doctors again if they had any other ideas on what had caused my situation. But they had no answers.

I added, "Maybe they were ghosts...."

A doctor replied, "You never know. Look at all that's out there now on the paranormal."

I was a little surprised by his open mindedness. While John went to get the car, I stayed in the waiting room and watched what was on television. Coincidentally, the show was about "Real Ghost Stories."

Once I was on the antibiotics I felt much better in general. Also, it killed all the Botox in my face. So the headaches stopped as well as the flu-like symptoms, my blurred vision, my neck-aches, the numbness in my hand, and the general aches and pains.

For several months I saw many more doctors looking for answers. I was tested for everything, including metal poisoning, but nothing was found. One doctor commented, "I don't know what happened to you. Do you have any ideas?"

One of my theories at that point was that it was the Botox. I had read many things about the Botox seeping out of the muscle and causing problems. One person even contracted encephalitis, which causes hallucinations and brain damage. There were a few other reports of Botox and hallucinations. It seemed too coincidental that possible side effects connected with Botox included headaches, neck-aches, general aches and pains, ear congestion, swollen glands, urinary tract infections, respiratory infections like the flu, nervousness, insomnia, fast heartbeat, blurred vision, and a drooping brow and lids. These were all things I had experienced. But the private doctor I was seeing did not feel I was given enough for this to happen. Some of the side effects were more connected to other more focused uses of the drug. For him it seemed a big jump to go to the experience I had. I was also living in a very damp city where flu-like symptoms were prevalent.

I went to a Jungian Psychiatrist who had studied at Duke University, where they have the largest psychic research facility in the country. He was the final doctor who examined me, so he had all the input and medical reports of all the other doctors. His diagnosis was that it was a combination of everything; extreme exhaustion, having been under extreme stress for a long period of time, the bladder infection (hallucinations are common in the elderly), possibly the Botox, my sensitive hearing to the constant noise outside, and the paranormal. He called it "A Perfect Storm" with all the variables. He also felt that it was entirely possible that I was picking up some information from "out there." And, like the other doctors, he ruled out schizophrenia and every other kind of mental disorder. And I was never prescribed any medication. I saw him for only a few sessions because he didn't feel I needed any more. He had adequate information for his diagnosis of the situation. Later I conferred with him after having a session with an intuitive. He listened, but mostly reconfirmed his diagnosis that it was a combination of things, including the paranormal. Then a strange thought hit me that I related to him.

"What if the way these spirits, or angels, or whatever they were, were going to try to help me was by providing me with this story? Maybe it wasn't random. It incorporated everything, even my music. It was cruel but made a good story." He nodded and smiled, understanding my logic and thought process, but did not comment.

27

LAYMEN'S DIAGNOSES

OME "NON-BELIEVERS" OF the paranormal and traditional thinkers thought I just finally, spontaneously, had a nervous breakdown. Hearing voices and being watched by cameras concealed in vents is pretty cliché for a person going crazy. Though, "Just because you're paranoid doesn't mean they aren't after you," wrote Joseph Heller in "Catch-22." In today's world, so many things are possible in technology with spyware that the concept of "Big Brother" watching is universally accepted. The idea of living a life in an urban environment and having total privacy is actually the "crazy" concept. But the real problem with the "nervous breakdown" theory is that I was happy. I wasn't depressed. I was in Venice. I had gotten out from under all the nightmares of my real estate disasters. I had gone through the critical stage of processing the death of my son. I was optimistic and looking forward. Sure, things weren't perfect yet, but they were improving. Generally, with a nervous breakdown you are overwhelmed and depressed. You've broken down.

Another eager-to-diagnose colleague suggested "The Truman Show Syndrome."

She had read a fascinating article about it in the "New Yorker." I had never heard of it nor seen "The Truman Show." After doing extensive research, I acknowledged that there were some similarities to my story, just as there were similarities to my story and mental illness or ghosts. But the diagnosis didn't explain the entire experience.

The "Truman Show Syndrome" is a new term doctors have concocted to define the delusion of some people who believe that their life is part of a reality show. Evidently, there has been an increase of this syndrome showing up in various psychiatrists' offices. They attribute it to being a reflection of our current time.

Delusions have evolved through the years and are a reflection of our culture. In earlier years, the paranoia focused on things such as being controlled by radio waves or having had microchips implanted in your brain. They were a reflection of current events, society, and fears at that time. Now, communication is instantaneous due to cell-phones. Technology has evolved so that accessing someone's private life isn't difficult, so delusions of "being watched" aren't so delusional. Also, since there has been an increase in popularity of reality shows, making an average person an instant star, as well as networking sites that allow people to project their life over the Internet instantaneously, as if their life is particularly noteworthy, delusions of self-importance are exacerbated. Although, unfortunately, not every Internet junkie will end up in a psychiatrists' office, their delusions of grandeur are no less disturbing than the delusions of the ones who do. For someone to believe that their average existence of going to work, to the gym, or to dinner, and their every thought along the way are so uniquely profound that they are internally driven to broadcast their lives around the globe is indeed crazy behavior.

The profile of people who generally develop "The Truman Show Syndrome" is a person who has problems interacting or socializing with others. They have a strong connection to the computer and television, and see it as a way to interact with people and be accepted. These inter-actions and cyber-relationships become their reality and not the interaction one on one with real human beings in person. There may be some exceptions but this is the general profile.

Although there was the similarity of having "the reality show" concept in my situation, I was also open to the ideas such as ghosts, experiments, abduction, a brain tumor, and that I spontaneously went insane. And yes, many of these options are the typical delusions of someone having a psychotic episode. But I am a "sensitive" which adds another dimension to a diagnosis. I also sanely questioned if I went insane and was logical about it all. Not one of my doctors considered this a diagnosis or a symptom of a disorder. One reason is that I simply did not fit the profile. I do not particularly like all the social networking opportunities and don't participate. I don't even like the telephone much. I prefer to meet people in person and talk and learn from others' experiences. I am very social. But the most compelling evidence to dispute this theory is that my experience lasted only within the duration of time I was living in the apartment. It began from the day I moved into the new apartment and ended the day I moved out. I had never had a similar episode before this time and I've never had another one since. I was also never given any medication to stop the voices. My belief that I was being watched was only at the very end of the whole experience. I overheard these people partying and speaking of other people for weeks. They would wake me up. This is more in line with a prank than a grandiose delusion. There was no plot. I know I am subjecting myself to many opinions. But I believe my situation was more complex than just attributing it to a simplified term for convenience sake.

❧❧❧

28

ALTERNATIVE DIAGNOSIS

STILL WANTING ANSWERS after seeing many doctors on two continents, I went to an intuitive, Jonna Rae Bartges. I did not seek out this situation, but it came to me. Evidently, my mother had mentioned a few things about my experience to a liberal minded friend of hers when I was seeing doctors. Of course, my mother has also witnessed many psychic dreams of mine that came true. Her friend gave her the book, "Psychic or Psychotic" by Jonna Rae Bartges, to pass on to me. Obviously, the title was extraordinarily coincidental with what I was going through. Even more coincidental was that Jonna happened to be in town for a little while, and not on one of her public speaking tours around the country. I was severely traumatized from my situation and was open to all possibilities. I knew that the paranormal was involved with my experience, but I was confused and needed clarification about it all. The doctors' explanations were still too vague for me. I needed more insight or validation. So, I made an appointment to meet with her. I quoted and paraphrased some of my reading.

I asked, "I'd like to know what happened to me in February and March."

Initially she assessed my energy. "Energetically, your whole body energy is pulsing, throbbing…. It's uncomfortable. It's as if you squeeze your finger and the blood keeps building and throbbing. You are very, very intuitive. Everything is hitting you without any kind of filter. You are trying to ground and feel logical but it is so overwhelming. You are not in your body. You are amassing all this power. You are standing in your power but you don't know what to do with everything."

That was indeed how I felt. Then she proceeded to tell me she was going to explain an image she picked up. She said it could be literal or symbolic.

"I see you cruising along in your car and everything was fine. Then you came to an abrupt stop. You somersaulted out and split in three directions…. As human beings, we have the ability to be multi-dimensional people. You can be aware of where you are in the past, present, and future; constantly tapping into the energy of these things simultaneously. You're getting information from somewhere but you don't know where it's coming from. It can be very disconcerting because you're so wide open and now there's not a direction for this energy to go to. You feel almost panicky sometimes."

I asked her to further clarify things.

"I see a brick wall. You came to an abrupt stop. You're getting feedback from different levels. You haven't been able to bring everything into alignment. Conflicting input…. It was externally directed. Not within you. External. Other people or forces blocked you. They imprinted their own personal ideas about it onto you."

"Were they alive or dead?"

"I would have to say dead. There were others' attitudes and ideas, outside judgments, fears from other people. You had different perspectives about the story. Every time, you tried to reanalyze it. See different ways to see it. But there were other peoples' judgments, expectations, demands, and them trying to control you. You almost had to stop in order to understand. It was confusing trying to integrate and get it all together."

Although I was "hearing" her partially, I was exhausted and having difficulty accepting what she was saying. I was looking for concrete words, but didn't feel like I was hearing them at that moment.

She reiterated, "It was outside stuff. It was not stuff coming from you. It's not something you created yourself. None of it was you. You are clairaudient."

Jonna related a story that was in her book about some entity that flew at her and attacked her in spirit. It was so unusual that for a moment she wondered if she'd created it. But she knew she did not. She impressed on me that there are many entities and dimensions "out there." Then she went into her meditative state to get more clear information for me.

"Are you familiar with negative thought forms?"

"No," I responded.

"If the whole country is worried about a recession then this thought becomes like a very big dark cloud. 'Sensitives' can feel and see this dark cloud. It is the same as if people have a strong belief about something. 'Sensitives' can feel it. You are incredibly psychic. But I don't see good boundaries around you. You need a spiritual seatbelt so you aren't so affected by these energies. You need to learn to refocus and ground yourself. You are clairaudient, clairsentient, clairvoyant.... You pick up energies of people.... You feel that it's about you, but it's empathy…. You feel it's about you, but it's not. It's about them…. You're feeling what they feel."

I could understand what she was saying because I felt like the whole situation had wiped me out. I was trying to get grounded again but my thoughts were still a little confused and fuzzy, absorbing all the possibilities.

"The energy around you is gold, but a muddy gold. There have been energies around you trying to have control over you. They were playing with you to take your power. This scares me … but, you can banish them. They were beings not on the 3 dimensional realm. When you have encounters with entities, don't give up your power…. Don't let them make you their pawn. Don't let things take your power and don't worry what people are thinking."

She also mentioned that at the time I was going through this, there were several solar flares that affected "sensitives," making them more "sensitive."

"Your experience was from people who had crossed over, negative thought forms, and beings from other dimensions. The stress and being a little sick made it hard to bring it all into alignment. Things happen to normal people. But some of us pick up all this stuff and we're not crazy. It's important to share your story. Some of us came here with a specific mission … to have people understand that this is not a psychotic breakdown, but it's having a finely honed "sensitivity" to all these things. These occurrences happen more frequently than people would like to believe. But you were given a whole story. You have a responsibility to share this story. I feel like you signed up to be a bridge. You're a leader. Stand up and do what you're supposed to…. You're the perfect person to share the story. Do something full screen in a surround sound kind of way … the way you've lived your life … super dramatic. Don't do anything halfway. People are hungry to get answers…. On one level you're nice and normal. But, on another level, you're being activated to share."

It was intriguing how she "understood" the extremes in my life. I related to her the song I'd written, "The Other Side of the Wall."

She laughed and added, "See, I picked up the wall." She continued to explain that more music would be coming to me.

After some thought, I realized that the walls in Venice were originally brick as well. Before we finished up, I had a few more questions.

"There was a woman I met in Venice. Her name was Trish. What do you think about her?" I asked.

Jonna went into her meditative state for a moment then returned.

"I don't see you're connected now."

"No, not really."

"I see the movie, 'The Roommate.' Do you know it?"

"No."

"It's about a girl who is impressed with a girl and wants to emulate everything about her. She was jealous. She saw you as her link to things ... maybe Nashville and Hollywood. She wanted to use you."

I asked another question, "Can ghosts read your mind?"

She answered, "Yes, they can pick up on your fears and play on that. Living people learn how to manipulate people in the same way. They will deliberately go after you and what your vulnerabilities can be ... if you let them. We have control over how much power we give over to them."

Time was up with my session. To conclude, she reiterated, "You need to restore your energy centers. You're not in your body. You're not grounded."

She followed with sharing a protection meditative prayer for me to use, so that I could become more grounded.

At the time of the reading, I didn't fully understand how what she was saying pertained to what I was asking.

My mind was fuzzy. I was also hung up on her first interpretation with the car hitting the wall. I wondered if, at first, she thought I had been in an automobile accident. Also, there are no cars in Venice. Even though she said at the time her vision could be symbolic, it didn't register. She did assure me, though, that when I listened back on the tape, it would all make sense.

Trying to make light of all my information I added, "I hope there won't be any other voices on the tape."

She laughed and said, "Well, I wouldn't be surprised."

It took a very long time for me to listen to the tape of this session again. I didn't want to relive that traumatic time of my life. I actually wasn't convinced of her abilities when I left that day. But, when I finally listened again, many months later, I was astonished at how clear and concise she was. She did answer all of my questions. Her comment of me being "open" that day was how I felt. It was as if I had been riding on the roof of a car at 80 miles an hour, with the wind thrashing around every part of my body. My senses were maxed out. I was exhausted and it was hard to absorb any more information clearly at that time. My ears were full and I was fuzzy. But I "got it" when I listened to the tape again, as she had said. I feel very fortunate that I was guided to her. She's an amazingly gifted person. Of course, this is just another opinion to my experience, but I feel a remarkable one.

While finishing the manuscript, I wrote to Jonna, telling her that I'd documented my story as she'd suggested. I included a portion of her response:

> "*Thank you for doing this! 'Coming out of the spiritual closet' is a gut-wrenching and terrifying decision. By sharing your story, you'll help countless others realize their own experiences really are not a fluke. You're bringing a collective truth into mainstream awareness. Congratulations!*"

❧❀❧

29

MY DIAGNOSIS

'M GOING TO approach this logically, even if many of the concepts are "out there." Firstly, I want to point out that I've been through too many extremes in my life to spontaneously fall apart. And realistically, people don't just spontaneously go insane for no reason. In my opinion "The Perfect Storm" theory was vague and didn't offer detailed explanations of how all the parts actually contributed. The storm elements did not seem so intense to create such a powerful "perfect storm," unless one of them was a strong contributor. I wanted to understand it more.

I know when I've been exhausted I receive more psychic information in my dreams. I'm too tired to keep a wall up. I think everything, including the Botox side effects, put me in an altered state, so I could hear more clearly the paranormal, whatever it was. The walls were down between dimensions. I was also exhausted from being kept up at night, so I was more able to be manipulated and confused with the changing stories. Though, I believe, I always made logical decisions based on the information I had.

When there is a belief about a situation, your mind accepts other information that supports the initial belief. I overheard conversations that people were following me and filming me. I have acute hearing that has consistently been trustworthy and verifiable. So, obviously, when I saw people watching me I assumed that they were likely with the show. There was no reason for me not to believe what I had heard. But I did periodically question this, because I knew that although it was plausible, it might not have been probable. In the same way, when people are reading my story they may formulate an opinion early on, based on their beliefs and life experiences, and overlook other ideas that I presented in the story. As an architect, I was always trained to look at all possibilities which I have tried to include.

From as early as Architecture School, I was accustomed to functioning on little sleep to meet deadlines. Much of my lifestyle that followed incorporated these "deadlines" or necessities to perform under pressure. My thinking was analytical and organized. And there was no "trigger" that would have set off the situation. The few bad experiences I encountered were nothing compared to what I had dealt with in the past. I was generally happy in Venice. If I were drugged or had some mental disorder, my speech would have been slurred or disorganized. I would have shown some physical signs or I would not be able to function in "the real world." People would have noticed strange behavior, particularly friends and family who have known me for a long time. But, to everyone, I seemed normal.

I believe it had to do with what was in that apartment. The duration of my experience started from as soon as I moved into that apartment and ended the day I moved out. This is the most significant element of the story. Most of the experiences were literally in the apartment, except at the end when things escalated and as I was leaving on the airplane. I didn't hear strange stories while I was walking around. I was out living a normal life and having normal conversations. I do not do drugs and there were long stretches when I wouldn't even drink alcohol. And they found nothing in my blood.

I believe there were good and evil beings/spirits/ entities in that building. Some were pranksters, some wanted to scare me, and some were nice, wanting to help me. And, once they knew I could partially hear them, they wanted me out and wanted to manipulate me. I also toyed with them when I staged the phone calls and faked an overdose, trying to outsmart them and get answers. This may have encouraged them to further manipulate me and to concoct their elaborate plan.

I heard laugh-out-loud jokes and stories that stemmed from a different culture and background than mine. There were historical facts that I didn't know and had to look up later and verify. And they were accurate. How would I know these things? I tried to tell my story, being as exact as possible with the dialog, but there were some things I didn't understand and did not include. Hearing about the diseases was new to me as well. Only a doctor could spew out that information. Many comments from British Superman were things I would not have asked for. So, how can you say that it stemmed from me? Also, he found my fanny pack. Maybe somewhere in my subconscious I knew it was there. But how would I have known that the suitcase had fallen over? They also stated inaccurate facts about me, like my age. How could that come from me? I knew how old I was. Almost all the personal information that was discussed about me was either documented on my website, from another web-site I visited, or from a conversation I had with someone, like Trish, while I was in Venice. Only British Superman came up with things that were private to me.

Everything I did was logical, based on the parameters of the information I was given. I tried to confront them, believing they were people. I lived a normal life, but heard voices and stories. And yes, later I could see some things that had to do with electronic equipment, like the television. It's a widely accepted concept that spirits can manipulate energy and electricity. Perhaps in my altered state I was also a little more clairvoyant. Or I would hear voices coming from people that were not the people talking. As ghosts, they could have been standing next to the real people.

For many years, starting from when I was very young, I would have dreams and sometimes nightmares of walking down these long dark corridors. And there were wooden walls and ramps. Sometimes I would be afraid, sometimes not. Sometimes I would be chased. What frightened me was that I couldn't see. I thought that it could possibly mean that I was going to be blind in the future. I had these dreams from when I was very young, until I had a revelation while working as an actress in my early 30's. I was often on sound stages, walking down black corridors while they were filming. It hit me one day—the feeling was the same as in the dreams. I was never chased, but sometimes it was very scary and I felt like someone could be following me. When I put it together, I thought and knew, "This is it!" Somehow, this was a part of my life path. And I had been dreaming about it my whole life. Once I'd made that connection, the recurring dreams, that had haunted me for so many years, stopped.

As I was writing this story, another dream I've never forgotten came to mind. I believe I was about 14 when I dreamed it. I was standing in a cavernous room, maybe like a small stadium or theatre, with all eyes on me. I was in the light and there was evil around me. I was standing up for myself, speaking out for good against evil. Then I recited the Lord's Prayer. It was a dream that has remained with me since then. Isn't it strange how it parallels the event of my standoff in the Basilica di San Giovanni e Paolo? Could that experience have been fated for my life?

Maybe British Superman was an angel; I don't know. But when I think of him, I think of the song, "What If God Was One of Us." All I know is that he was there for me, offering love and support. Yes, "his story" changed constantly and he never showed up physically with help. But what didn't change was that he was always there for me. He gave me hope, strength, and encouragement to triumph over the mean ones who were beating me down. He changed my focus. As the British woman said, "All that really matters is a little kindness."

Another situation came to mind months after listening to my "reading" again from Jonna. I had a distant cousin who was my age who passed away just before I went to Venice. I rarely saw her, but was very close to her aunts. They were not sure of her cause of death. She had been ill just before her passing. Some were concerned it was suicide, but there was no evidence to support this at the time. I knew she had some problems growing up, as was told to me, but I wasn't completely filled in. Early on, she was a ballerina and had an eating disorder. She also had drug and alcohol problems at times, as well as depression. Part of it revolved around her pain from fibromyalgia. People go through many things in life and it was her personal business. I only had a few updates about her over the years, without all the details.

Months after my return from Venice, I was told that she suffered from severe malnutrition and other organ complications from her behavior over the years. When I thought about what Jonna said about me being an empath, I wondered if I could have been picking up some of her story that was discussed amongst my relatives when I was away. Maybe this was a negative thought form. My experience dealt with several of her issues.

I also recently became aware of a profound historic paranormal story on the island of Poveglia, between Venice and Lido, in the lagoon. This Venetian island is supposedly considered "the most haunted island in the world" and referred to as "the island of madness." It became a quarantine station for plague victims. The bodies would be burned and dumped in pits. Anyone suspected of having the plague was dragged out of their house and taken to the island and burned. The homes of the victims were burned as well. A prison was on the island and an insane asylum was utilized later. Evidently, an unethical doctor secretly did experiments on some of the patients and performed lobotomies. Years later, the doctor claimed he was being driven crazy by ghosts. One day, he went up to the bell tower or was "controlled" to go there and he jumped off to his death. Some say he was thrown off by spirits. More than 100,000 people were buried on the island. It has been reported that the waves sometimes uncover human remains. People have been afraid to go to the island, with many reports of screams and other paranormal encounters.

A British couple supposedly purchased the island to make a holiday home. On their first night there, their child encountered a freak situation, having part of his face ripped and requiring several stitches. They never went back. Obviously, they weren't welcomed there. Now, Italy is auctioning off the island to cover some of its debt. I am not certain if the area of Venice where I was staying had plague victims that were dragged to the island or not. I also don't know all the details of the doctor's experiments with mental patients and how they ended up in his asylum. But it is an interesting story to ponder, that could possibly be related to my story.

There were always a few gleeful whisperings, that I would hear periodically, saying, "She'll be gone in a few days." These voices were fainter than broadcast, like the others. It was obvious that this was a strong opinion behind my story. Whatever was behind these voices wanted me out of the apartment. Maybe this is the answer to the entire experience.

The element of seeing the horse and cart on the mainland, which disappeared as the plane took off, suggests that somehow I was connected to a different time period. Who knows, maybe that area of town, that is centuries old, had some portal that somehow I became connected with, and I was living different time periods simultaneously. The carts with wooden wheels I'd heard in the early morning could have also been from the other time period.

Maybe, as my psychiatrist said, my experience was a combination of many variables. But I believe the paranormal had the strongest influence.

30

HOW I'VE CHANGED

I DO WISH THERE were concrete answers for what happened to me. But, I guess there is much in life where we have to practice faith. As one doctor told me, "Just try to forget about it and move on with your life." That's a pretty simplistic dismissal. But, in a way, it's all you can do. But, I don't want to forget it. Maybe it was a gift. Look at Moses, Joan of Arc, William Blake, Socrates and other famous people and prophets who have heard things. These weren't voices in my head. They were out of my head on the other side of the wall. Or they were coming from another direction, other part of the room, in the room above me, or below me. But they were from "the other side of the wall." From a philosophical perspective, I always saw "the other side of the wall" from their conversations. We only understand good from seeing the presence of evil. I heard both sides. But, also, I saw how miraculous life is. It is the way most of my life has been. Life can change in an instant, either for good or bad.

I once had a friend who was taking care of her mother who had lupus. Her name was Susan. She was one of the most positively evolved people I have ever known. It was tragic that she was saddled with that responsibility when her father, who had a lot of money, couldn't deal with it. Her mother would have seizures where Susan never knew how it would turn out. Would they be going to the hospital? Would it be the end? Or would it be over and back to normal? She never knew, just like the unanswered questions of a 911 call-person. She was always on the edge. But, she saw it through each time. She would say to me her philosophy on life, "If things are going bad, just wait five minutes." And she'd laugh. I couldn't understand how she could laugh. But I grew to understand that she had a profound understanding of life. One minute things can be dark, and the next there is light. There is always "the other side of the wall."

Obviously, I was severely traumatized by the situation. When I hear people talking, I get nervous until I've checked to see if they are there. Of course, I still question if somehow it can happen again. But I just have to have faith that if it does I'll be able to deal with it, like I did before. Now, I have a little more knowledge about it all. And maybe I'll just "wait five minutes," knowing things do change. One of the true miracles in life is that we can always count on change.

❦

31

MY RETURN TO VENICE

I DID RETURN TO Venice. I love the city and I needed to face my fears. I even eventually went back to the area around where I lived … with friends. To be honest, it still frightens me to go near the flat. I usually run by. Strangely, I ended up in an apartment on the calle, "Borgolocco," nearby, but a canal away. At first, when I read the address, I was frightened because I thought it meant "Crazy Street," knowing "loco" means "crazy" in Spanish. I thought the forces were somehow bringing me back. But, thank God, that's not how it translated in Italian. That's what I rationalized anyway. I avoided taking that apartment for a while, but somehow all my other options kept falling through. So I took it. And, wouldn't you know, around the corner from the place was a bar called "The Crazy Bar." It was spooky, but I faced my fears and never heard any voices from people that weren't there again. Actually, maybe being in the general vicinity of the other place helped with confronting them.

Just before Christmas, December 22rd, I was mugged and beaten at night near the Rialto Bridge. This was unusual because, generally, Venice is very safe at all hours. But it was late and I had my hands full from Christmas shopping that day. I was hit from behind and my hand was broken while clinging to my new boyfriend's Christmas gifts. I saved the gifts, but my assailant stole my purse in the struggle. It was traumatic, crying for help that brutal night and, later, spending twelve hours with the police. But the worst part of it was that my new boyfriend, who was a chef at the Palazzina Grassi, decided he had enough obligations, particularly at Christmas, and didn't help me. The police originally tried to reach him through the Palazzina Grassi, but the hotel did not locate him. He lived a ten-minute walk away and didn't care to even check on me, knowing I was injured, even after I begged him for help. For all he knew I could have been dying alone in my apartment with internal injuries. Other friends were out of town for Christmas and not reachable. I didn't call my family, because my brother had been in the hospital with cancer and my mother had been ill from worrying about my brother. My boyfriend not showing up was quite ironic because he was the one who asked if we could spend Christmas together, and was the reason why I was shopping for presents for him last minute to put under my tree. Every few hours he told me he would be over to see me, for days, but he never showed up. I spent Christmas alone with no food, no money, broken, and wondering if the person who had my purse and house keys could break in. It was the worst Christmas I had ever had. And, unfortunately, my right writing hand was permanently damaged from waiting too long to go to the hospital because I was waiting for him, and I didn't know if I needed cash. But, even with that much drama and anguish, the reality show wasn't there filming…. So, in a way, that was positive. I confirmed that I could handle extreme situations, which further supported the theory that my former experience was external and did not stem from me. Another positive outcome was that I found out what a horrible person I was dating early on. As a friend stated politely, "He was a selfish prick!" I did find out that he was only separated, and not divorced as he had told me. But he was not even man enough to be a friend to me. It makes you wonder what kind of energy he puts into his artistic creations as a chef, which people consume….

On the bright side, and not a surprise, Lucio was there for me. He had helped me do the shopping for him, and he was there later when I needed a friend. I gave him one of the gifts he had helped me pick out.

I have also learned a long overdue lesson—words have power. They can be healing, or they can be dangerous tools for deception. For instance, when a man tells you up front, "I'm a good guy, you'll see ..." even though I would love to be proven wrong, he probably isn't a good guy and you will never see that he is. Still, I always like to believe that people are telling me the truth, even though I've endured great heartache from believing in people with beautiful things to say. Mountains can be moved by someone who has someone who believes in him. Believing in someone gives them the opportunity to rise to the occasion to be their best self. This is a gift. But not everyone appreciates this "gift" and will use it to their advantage.

In general, I've met many human angels in Venice. Two sisters, Carolina and Martina, at the Hotel Hesperia, an extraordinary family run hotel, have been like my own sisters. They have helped with many things to get me adjusted into life in Venice, as well as offered sage advice. Franco and his family have been invaluable. I've met many artists and people in music who have been encouraging and supportive. Even the police stayed in touch and were helpful in other situations.

As for Trish, well, she pretty much disappeared out of

my life once I left Venice the first time. She wrote me once in response to an email, but never returned any other correspondence I sent. She has been friendly when I've seen her in public, but is usually brief and scurries off. I was a little disappointed that she circulated my story after I left the first time. But, once I returned, everyone pretty much forgot about it. They always saw me acting normally, anyway. She was the only one I had told about the voices.

My situation on Borgolocco deteriorated with my landlords. I'm not sure why exactly, except that THEY were likely crazy. They were more interested in getting more money than having a good tenant for a long time. And they were uncomfortable about me being an American, I think. But it was helpful to be in the area of the other flat to heal and to write this book. And, coincidentally, I finished the first draft just before I moved out.

When I concluded that I couldn't handle the shenanigans of my landlords any longer, I searched the properties for rent. There was a new listing of this magical place, with a view on the water, in Murano. I had not even considered living in Murano because I liked being central. But it was such an intriguing photo that seemed to call out to me, so I had to see it. Coincidentally, a friend called from California who wanted to visit the day before the showing. She was in real estate and I had not seen her in more than 10 years. She was French and also very spiritual. She and her friend accompanied me to the showing. They were both blown away, saying that the energy was positive, flowed well, and wasn't trapped—a typical California comment that made me happy. They advised me to take it. It also reminded me of Montecito, where she lived, or Laguna Beach or Hibiscus Island, where I had lived. I had not been to Murano in some years, but it seemed to be one of the best kept secrets of Venice. It's a place filled with artists and imagination, upscale restaurants, boat enthusiasts, and everyday local people. There are some tourists, but no large tour groups. Historically, the island had summer palaces when the island was filled with orchids and gardens. And, due to the fear of fires in Venice, the glass blowers and factories moved to Murano. These artists, famous throughout the world for centuries for glass, were part of the upper crust of Venice. The positive creative energy there did feel right for me.

Murano is an idyllic village. When it's warm, the children strip down at the bridges and jump into the canals, screaming and giggling. It's a perfect picture of a time that no longer exists in many places. Everyone knows everyone. After being forced to sell my house on Hibiscus Island in Florida, I was now living on the pristine Murano Island.

You have to wonder what powers or spirits were working together to orchestrate this life correction.

To everyone I've dated since the event, I first ask if he's ever died before. Of course, it confuses them. But you never know....

One day, I was having a Prosecco at the Hotel Danieli and I heard some British voices behind me. I turned around and saw a small group of people. This one man was sizzling hot. He was lean with dark hair and light eyes. He had proper mannerisms, but was sexy and not stiff. He got up and came over to the bar beside me and ordered a drink. I was very nervous as he was so attractive. I tried not to stare, but his energy seemed to pour over into my personal space. It was warm and magnetic. So I would glance then look away, not to be too obvious. He turned, stared at me, and just smiled without a flinch. He was very confident. I was frozen and couldn't say a thing, and just gave a smile. He lingered for far longer than a quick glance, just staring. Then he turned and headed back to his group. That encounter has stayed with me. We said nothing to one another, but it was a moment frozen in time. It was like the Prendergast painting of Venice with the umbrellas over the bridge. The umbrellas were the shield that held that moment of perfection of the era in place, and frozen so it couldn't drift away. That moment, not even a weekend, was grounded by the perfect historic Hotel Danieli. It is the same hotel, when at Carnevale, you have to question when seeing everyone in costume in the dim lights, who is from the present or who could possibly be from a different century, as they are all dressed the same.

32

CONCLUSION

A FUNNY THING HAPPENED when I was packing to leave to go back to Venice. A friend connected to the entertainment industry, who knew about my experience, said to me, "I'm just a little curious. Would you be surprised if you returned to Italy and turned on the television and saw yourself on that reality show?"

I hesitated, thinking it through, and said, "No.... But I'm not crazy."

"I know you're not. They have the technology to do everything that happened to you. But wouldn't that be amazing? To have gone through all that and to find out in the end it was real?"

I shared an understanding smile and concluded, "It's probably been airing in China."

But, this is my advice if you ever visit Venice: If you hear voices upstairs, downstairs, beside you, or outside, basically on the other side of the wall, and you check and there's no one there, assume they are probably talking about you. But don't listen. Ignore them. Don't fuel them. And if they torment you and keep you up at night, or move or hide things (a friend here explained her experience with that happening in a place she rented), just move. It's an incredible city, maybe with many dimensions still occurring simultaneously. But it's a heavy city. So, just move and enjoy your stay, and experience the magic and love of Venice. You will feel love everywhere once you change your focus.

Lightning Source UK Ltd.
Milton Keynes UK
UKOW03f2325120914

238472UK00002B/11/P

9 780990 500100